Leatherworking 101

A Comprehensive Step-By-Step Beginner's Guide to Mastering the Art of Leatherworking and Creating Beautiful Leather Pieces

Introduction

Would you love to master the captivating art of leatherworking and create beautiful leather pieces like belts, bags, and more?

Have you tried to learn about leatherworking but feel overwhelmed by the complexities of leatherworking?

Would you want to get a comprehensive resource that breaks down the essential steps and techniques in a way that's easy to follow?

If so, then you've come to the right place.

Leatherworking doesn't have to be a daunting craft reserved for experts. With the right approach and step-by-step instructions, anyone can learn and excel in this art form.

In this all-inclusive guide, we have carefully crafted a comprehensive resource to help you embark on your leatherworking journey with confidence. Whether you're a complete novice or have dabbled in leatherworking without much success, this book will take you from the basics to mastering the art of creating stunning leather pieces.

Here's a glimpse of what you'll learn:

- The different types, grades, and characteristics of leather so you can choose the suitable materials for your projects
- The essential tools and materials needed for leatherworking so you can have everything you need to get started
- How to set up a dedicated leatherworking workspace, optimizing your environment for creativity and productivity
- The basic techniques and terminology of leatherworking so you can have a solid foundation for your leather crafting endeavors

But that's not all! We go beyond the fundamentals and delve into more advanced topics, including:

- How to select the right leather for your projects based on quality, durability, and aesthetics
- Preparing your leather through cleaning, conditioning, and stiffening techniques for optimal results
- Softening and stretching techniques to achieve the desired texture and flexibility in your leather

- Cutting, stitching, and assembly techniques to take your leatherworking skills to the next level

And that's just the beginning! We also explore:

- Embellishment and decoration techniques, such as embossing, carving, and dyeing, so that you can add intricate designs and personal touches to your creations

- Finishing techniques that bring out the beauty and durability of your leather pieces

- Essential care and maintenance tips to ensure your products stand the test of time

But this book goes beyond just teaching you the technical aspects of leatherworking. It's about embracing the joy of creation, the satisfaction of bringing your ideas to life, and the pride of crafting something truly remarkable.

I believe that as you desire to embark on this journey to learn about leatherworking, you may have more questions running through your mind like:

How long will it take to learn leatherworking?

Can I practice leatherworking at home?

Are there any safety considerations I should be aware of?

What if I don't have access to specific tools or materials?

How can I troubleshoot common challenges or mistakes in leatherworking?

Rest assured; we have you covered. Throughout this book, we address these questions and more, providing practical guidance, troubleshooting tips, and insights to support you on your leatherworking journey. We aim to make learning leatherworking enjoyable, accessible, and rewarding for readers.

Don't let uncertainty hold you back. Take the leap, follow our guidance, and unlock your full potential in the captivating art of leatherworking. Your journey starts here, and we're here to guide you every step of the way.

If you have a burning desire to learn leatherworking and a passion for creating unique and timeless pieces, then "Leatherworking 101" is the perfect resource. No matter your background or previous experience, our detailed instructions, helpful tips, and inspiring projects will empower you to unleash your creativity and achieve outstanding results.

With this book's comprehensive guidance and step-by-step instructions, you can finally fulfill your dreams of mastering leatherworking and creating beautiful pieces that showcase your creativity and craftsmanship.

So, if you're ready to unlock your creativity, develop a new skill, and create stunning leather pieces that will be cherished for years, don't wait another moment. Start your leatherworking journey today.

Your adventure in leatherworking begins now!

Table of Contents

Section 1: Getting Started with Leatherworking

Chapter 1: Understanding Leather: Types, and Characteristics

Before diving into leatherworking, it's essential to understand the different types of leather available. Each type has unique qualities and characteristics, making it suitable for various projects.

Types of Leather

Here are some common types of leather:

- **Full-Grain Leather**

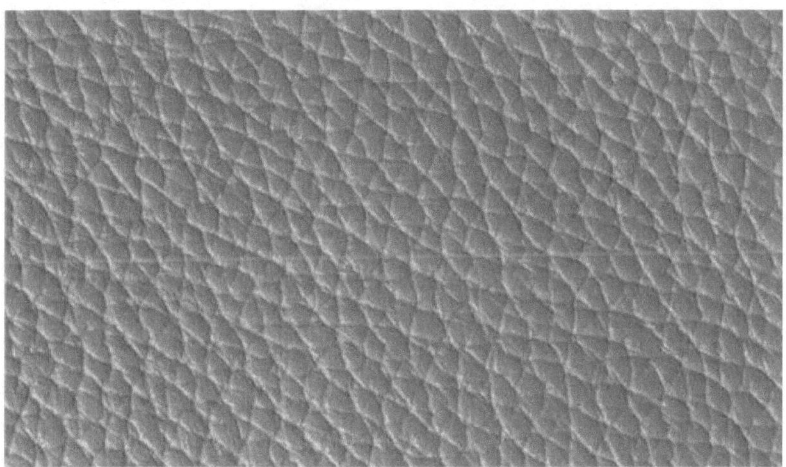

Full-grain Leather 1

Full-grain leather is ***considered the highest quality and most durable*** hence more expensive than other types of leather. It is made from the hide's top layer and retains the natural grain and markings, providing strength, longevity, and a beautiful aging process.

When you hold a piece of full-grain leather, you'll notice its rugged and natural appearance. You can feel the texture of the genuine grain and observe the presence of unique markings, scars, and wrinkles. These imperfections give the leather character and authenticity.

Full-grain leather is thick and sturdy, offering durability and longevity and making it suitable for projects. As you handle it, you may feel its weight and robustness.

Full-grain leather is available in various colors, from classic earth tones to vibrant hues. Depending on the desired aesthetic, its finish options can vary from matte to glossy or even distressed.

Let's explore the cleaning method of full-grain leather:

- ✓ Start by removing loose dirt and dust from the surface using a soft brush or lint-free cloth.
- ✓ Dampen a clean cloth or sponge with a mild leather cleaner specifically formulated for full-grain leather.
- ✓ In a circular motion, gently wipe the leather, focusing on any soiled areas or stains. Avoid excessive rubbing or scrubbing, as it can damage the leather.
- ✓ Wipe the leather with a damp cloth after cleaning to remove any residue from the cleaner.
- ✓ Allow the leather to air dry naturally, away from direct heat sources or sunlight.
- ✓ Once dry, apply a leather conditioner to restore moisture and keep the leather supple.

Please see Figure *(Full-grain Leather 1)* above for a visual representation.

- **Top-Grain Leather**

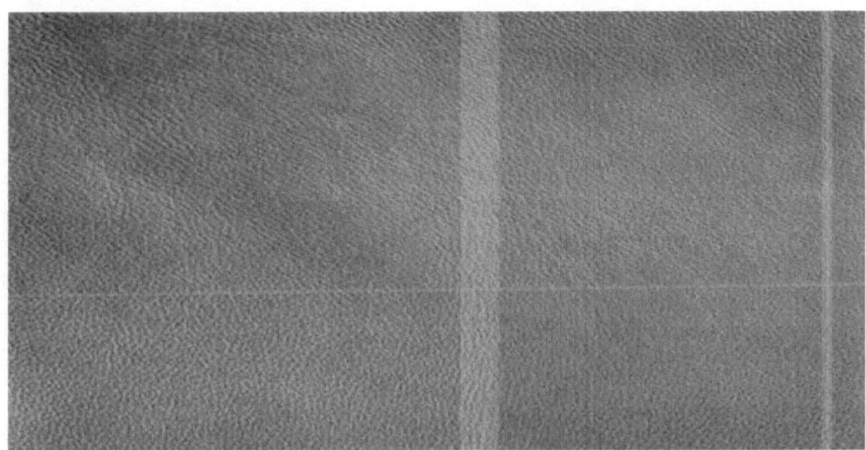

Top-grain Leather 1

Top-grain leather is ***slightly lower in quality and lighter in weight than full-grain leather*** but is still widely used in leatherworking projects. It is made by splitting the hide's top layer and removing imperfections.

When you hold a piece of top-grain leather, you'll notice that it has a refined and smooth surface that makes it versatile for different finishes. It feels soft, supple, and luxurious to the touch.

Top-grain leather ***is more uniform***, unlike full-grain leather, without prominent imperfections or natural markings. The surface is sleek and even, providing a consistent texture throughout the leather.

Top-grain leather's price can vary depending on the specific grade and treatment. We will not focus so much on the grades for this guide because that's a bit advanced for beginners. It is generally more affordable compared to full-grain leather.

Let's explore the cleaning method of top-grain leather:

- ✓ Similar to full-grain leather, begin by removing loose dirt and dust with a soft brush or cloth.
- ✓ Dampen a clean cloth or sponge with a mild leather cleaner suitable for top-grain leather.
- ✓ Focusing on any stains or soiled areas, gently wipe the leather surface. Avoid excessive pressure or scrubbing.
- ✓ To remove any cleaner residue after cleaning, wipe the leather with a damp cloth.
- ✓ Allow the leather to air dry naturally, away from direct heat or sunlight.

✓ Once dry, apply a leather conditioner to replenish moisture and maintain the leather's softness.

Please refer to the image (*Top Grain Leather 1*) above for visual representation.

- **Genuine Leather**

Genuine Leather 1

Genuine leather refers to leather made from natural animal hides. It ***encompasses both full-grain and top-grain leather and other lower-quality variations***. The specific layer used in genuine leather is not specified. The price, weight, quality, and durability of genuine leather can vary depending on its grade and treatment, making it versatile and suitable for various projects.

When you hold a piece of genuine leather, you may notice characteristics that resemble full-grain and top-grain leather, depending on the specific grade and treatment applied.

Genuine leather can range from thick and robust to smoother and softer textures. The surface appears more consistent without significant imperfections or natural grain patterns. Color options and finish treatments for genuine leather also vary, allowing various choices to suit different design preferences. The color and finish can enhance your projects' overall aesthetics and style.

Overall, genuine leather offers versatility in price, weight, quality, durability, texture, and appearance. It provides options for different project requirements and personal preferences, making it popular among leather enthusiasts.

Let's explore the cleaning method of genuine leather:

Genuine leather encompasses a wide range of leather types, including ***corrected grain leather, split leather, and other variations***. The cleaning method can vary depending on the specific type of genuine leather, but here is the general way to clean it:

- ✓ Start by gently removing loose dirt and dust from the surface using a soft brush or cloth.

- ✓ If there are stains or spills, refer to the appropriate cleaning method based on the specific type of genuine leather. For example, corrected grain leather can be cleaned similarly to top-grain leather, while split leather may require specialized cleaners.
- ✓ Follow the recommended cleaning instructions for the particular type of genuine leather you are working with.
- ✓ To remove any residue after cleaning, wipe the leather with a clean, damp cloth.
- ✓ Allow the leather to air dry naturally, away from direct heat or sunlight.
- ✓ Consider applying a suitable leather conditioner or protective product to maintain its quality and appearance, depending on the type of genuine leather.

Please refer to the image (*Genuine Leather 1*) above:

- **Bonded Leather**

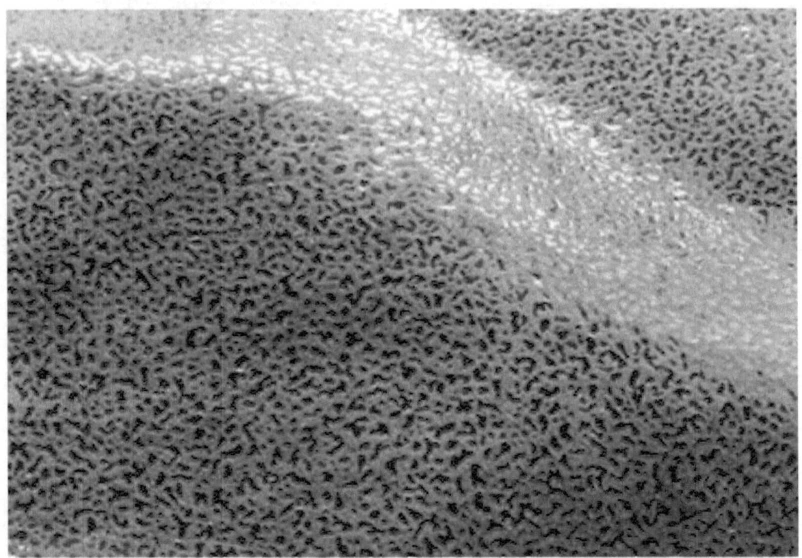

Bonded Leather 1

Bonded leather is ***created by bonding together leftover leather scraps using adhesives***. It is more affordable, making it a common choice for projects that do not require high levels of strength or longevity. However, it is generally less durable and does not possess the same qualities as full-grain or top-grain leather.

When you hold bonded leather, you'll notice that it feels different from genuine or top-grain leather. It often has a smooth and uniform surface, lacking natural grain patterns. Bonded leather is also typically thinner and lighter in weight.

Its texture may feel slightly artificial due to bonding small leather scraps with adhesives.

Bonded leather is often manufactured with a specific color and finish in mind. The color options for bonded leather can be diverse, ranging from solid colors to patterns or embossed designs. The finish of bonded leather is typically uniform and can have a glossy or matte appearance.

Let's explore the cleaning method of bonded leather:

- ✓ Begin by wiping the bonded leather surface with a soft, damp cloth to remove any surface dust or debris.
- ✓ For stains or spills, use a mild soap and water solution. Apply a small amount of the solution to a clean cloth and gently blot the stained area.
- ✓ Avoid excessive moisture and rubbing, as bonded leather is more susceptible to damage.
- ✓ To remove any soap residue after cleaning, wipe the surface with a clean, damp cloth.
- ✓ Allow the bonded leather to air dry naturally, away from direct heat sources.
- ✓ Once dry, you can apply a bonded leather conditioner or protective spray to enhance its appearance and durability.

Please refer to the image *(Bonded Leather 1)* above for a visual representation.

Selecting the Right Leather for Your Projects

When selecting the right leather for your projects, evaluating your requirements and intended use is crucial. Consider the specific characteristics and qualities that are important for your project.

Here are some key points to keep in mind:

- **Determine What You Are Making**

Consider the type of leather item you want to create, such as a bag, wallet, footwear, or garment. Different projects have different requirements, and certain leather types are better suited for specific items.

For example:

✓ Bags and footwear: Full-grain leather is often preferred for its durability and strength, making it suitable for heavy-duty items that require longevity and structural integrity.

✓ Wallets and small accessories: Top-grain leather or softer variations of genuine leather can provide the flexibility and suppleness needed for these smaller items.

- ✓ Garments: Soft and lightweight leather, such as lambskin or Nappa leather, is commonly used for garments as it offers comfort and ease of movement.

- **Assess Durability**

If your project requires high durability, such as for a bag or a pair of boots, choose leather known for its strength and ability to withstand wear and tear. With its natural grain and rugged appearance, full-grain leather is an excellent choice for durable projects.

- **Evaluate Flexibility**

For projects that require flexibility, like gloves or garments, opt for leather types that are supple and have good drapes. Top-grain leather or softer variations of genuine leather might be suitable for these applications.

- **Consider Aesthetics**

The appearance of the leather is an essential factor to consider. Some projects may benefit from a more natural and rustic look, while others require a sleek and refined finish. Full-grain leather adds character and authenticity with its unique grain patterns and imperfections, ideal for projects embracing a rugged aesthetic. Top-grain leather offers a smoother and more consistent appearance, suitable for projects prioritizing a polished and sophisticated look.

- **Specific Qualities**

Consider additional qualities such as water or scratch resistance, depending on your project's needs. With its natural oils, full-grain leather can resist water, making it suitable for moisture-sensitive items. Look for leather with a protective finish or natural resistance to scratches for scratch resistance.

Remember, there is no one-size-fits-all answer for the best leather for every project. It's essential to evaluate your project's unique requirements and prioritize the characteristics that matter most to you.

By considering factors such as project purpose, durability, flexibility, aesthetics, and specific qualities, you can make an informed decision and select the ideal leather for your project.

Chapter 2: Essential Tools for Leatherworking

Regarding leatherworking, having the right tools is essential for achieving professional and high-quality results.

Let's explore some of the critical tools in detail:

Cutting Tools

- **Utility Knife**

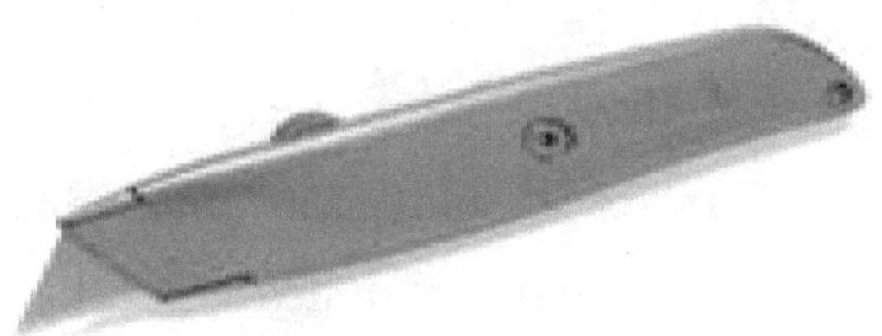

This versatile tool has a sharp, retractable blade for cutting leather into desired shapes and sizes. The adjustable blade allows you to control the depth of the cut, making it useful for various thicknesses of leather. The utility knife provides precision and clean cuts, whether you're trimming edges, cutting straight lines, or removing excess material.

- **Rotary Cutter**

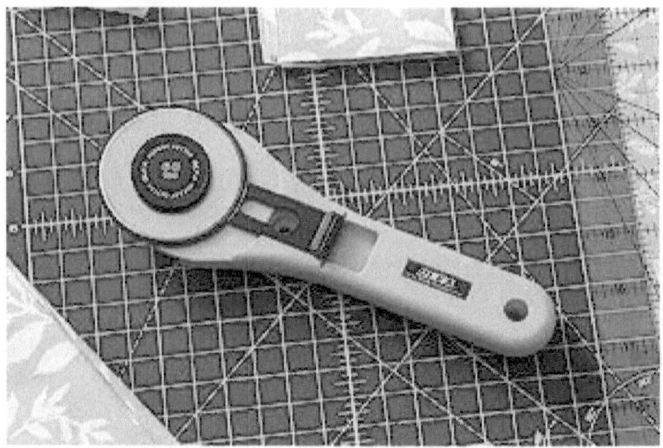

This tool features a circular blade that rolls smoothly along the leather surface, making it ideal for cutting straight lines and curves with precision and ease. The ergonomic design offers comfort and control, reducing hand fatigue during extended cutting sessions. The rotary cutter is particularly effective when working with thinner or delicate leathers, ensuring clean and accurate cuts.

- **Leather Scissors**

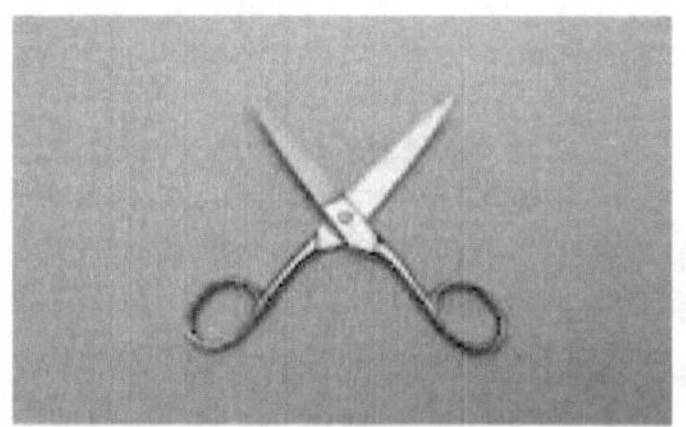

These sharp and sturdy scissors are designed for cutting leather and offer clean and accurate cuts. They are instrumental when cutting smaller pieces or intricate details that require more maneuverability than a knife or rotary cutter can provide. Leather scissors often have serrated or notched blades, which grip the leather securely to prevent slippage and ensure precise cutting.

- **Leather Splitter**

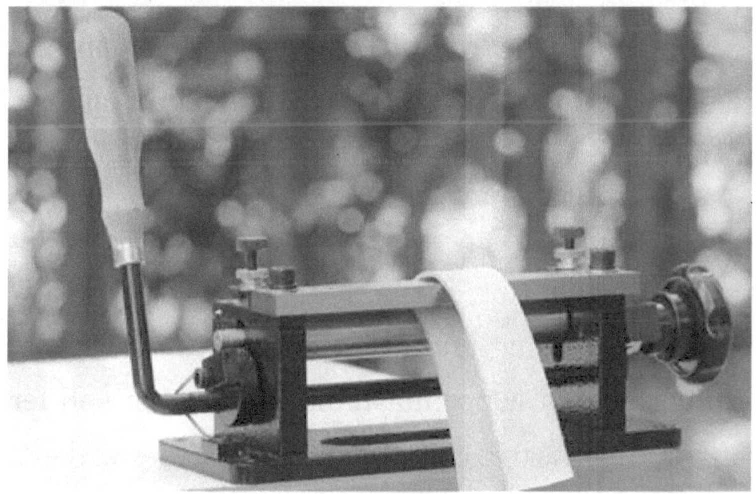

A leather splitter, also known as ***a leather skiver or leather paring machine***, is a specialized tool used in leatherworking to thin or shave down the thickness of leather hides. It is a valuable instrument for creating more delicate and flexible leather pieces with uniform thickness.

The leather splitter consists of a sharp blade positioned at an adjustable angle. Leatherworkers can feed the leather through the machine, and as it passes over the blade, a thin layer is removed, resulting in a slimmer and more even piece of leather. This process is particularly useful for projects that require thinner leather, such as making fine leather bookbinding, watch straps, or other intricate leather accessories.

Using a leather splitter allows for greater leatherworking precision, enabling leatherworkers to achieve consistent thickness throughout the hide. This level of control is essential when working on projects that demand precise measurements and a more refined finish.

However, as a beginner, it's essential to exercise caution while using a leather splitter, as the sharp blade is potentially hazardous. Proper training and safety measures are crucial when handling this tool. Once mastered, the leather splitter becomes an indispensable asset in the leatherworker's toolkit, enhancing the quality and versatility of their leather projects.

Now, let’s move to the stitching tools:

Stitching Tools

They include:

- **Stitching Awl**

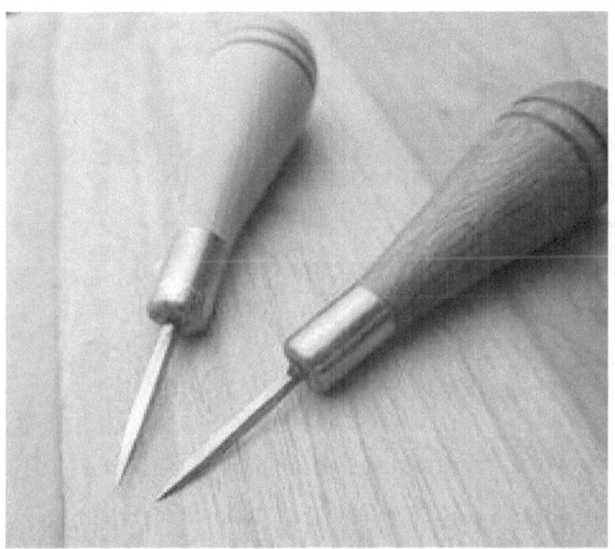

This is a pointed tool used for creating holes in the leather for stitching. It lets you efficiently and accurately mark stitching lines and patterns on the leather surface. The awl's sharp tip pierces through the leather with minimal effort, creating consistent and evenly spaced holes for hand stitching. This tool is especially helpful when working with thicker leather or multiple layers.

- **Needles**

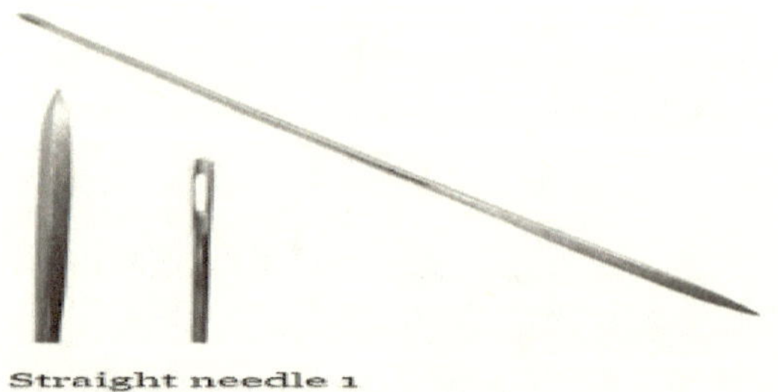

Straight needle 1

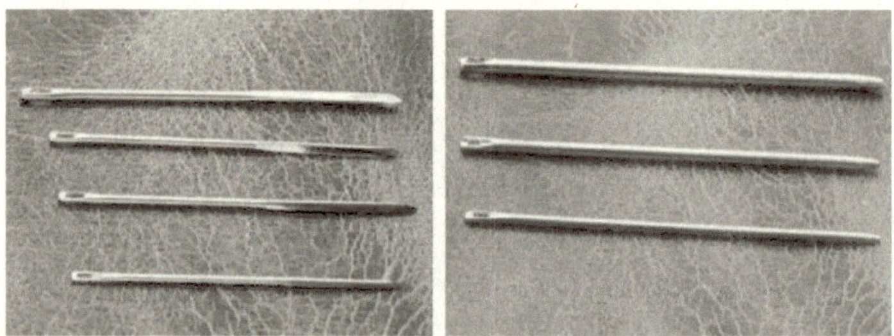

Leather needles come in various sizes and types, each serving a specific purpose in leatherworking.

For example, ***straight needles*** are commonly used for general stitching and accommodate different thread thicknesses.

Glover's needles, on the other hand, have a triangular point, making it easier to penetrate thicker leather. In comparison, ***harness needles*** have a rounded point and are suitable for heavier leathers and stitching belts or straps.

Choosing the right needle ensures smooth stitching and minimizes the risk of needle breakage or damage to the leather.

- **Thread**

Choosing the right thread is crucial for achieving strong, durable, visually appealing leatherworking stitches. The choice of a thread significantly ***impacts your stitched leather projects' overall quality and longevity***. One popular option in leatherworking is waxed nylon thread.

Let's look at the different types of threads used in leatherworking:

✓ ***Waxed Nylon Thread***

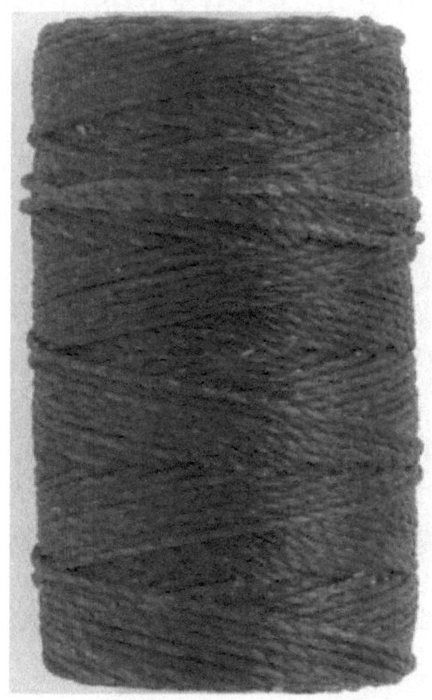

It is highly regarded for its exceptional strength, durability, and resistance to wear and tear. The wax coating on the thread enhances its durability, providing a protective layer that guards against abrasion and fraying. Additionally, the wax helps the thread glide smoothly through the needle holes, reducing friction and preventing tangling or breakage during stitching.

As a result, waxed nylon thread is commonly used for creating secure and long-lasting stitches on leather, making it an ideal choice for various leather items such as:

1. ***Bags and purses***: The strong and durable nature of waxed nylon thread makes it suitable for stitching together the various panels and components in bags and purses, ensuring the seams are secure and can withstand weight and usage.

2. ***Belts***: Waxed nylon thread is often used for stitching belt loops, attaching buckles, and securing the ends of belts, as it provides the necessary strength and durability to withstand tension and daily wear.

3. ***Wallets:*** Wallets require sturdy stitches to hold together multiple layers of leather and provide longevity. Waxed nylon thread is ideal for stitching wallets, ensuring the edges and compartments remain secure.

4. ***Leather accessories***: Waxed nylon thread is commonly used for various leather accessories, such as keychains, bracelets, and small leather items that require strong and durable stitches.

✓ ***Polyester Thread***

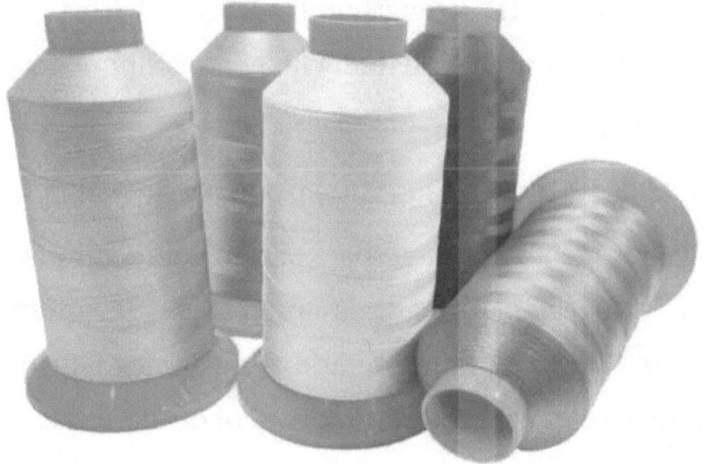

A polyester thread is a synthetic thread known for its strength, durability, and resistance to various elements. It is a popular choice for leatherworking due to its ***ability to withstand UV rays, mildew, and abrasion***. Polyester threads are available in multiple colors, allowing you to match or contrast with your leather project's design. It provides a polished and professional finish to your stitched leather pieces.

Polyester thread offers excellent tensile strength, ensuring your stitches remain secure and long-lasting.

It is particularly suitable for the following applications:

1. ***Upholstery***: Polyester thread is ideal for stitching leather upholstery for furniture, car seats, and other interior applications. Its strength and ability to withstand frequent use make it a reliable choice for upholstery projects.

2. ***Outdoor gear:*** When it comes to leather items used in outdoor gear, such as tents, backpacks, and camping equipment, polyester thread is preferred. It offers resistance to UV rays, mildew, and abrasion, ensuring that the stitches can withstand the rigors of outdoor use.

3. ***Leather footwear:*** Polyester thread is commonly used for stitching leather shoes, boots, and sandals. Its strength and durability suit withstanding footwear's daily wear and movement.

4. ***Heavy-duty leather projects***: Projects that require heavy-duty stitching, such as leather armor or industrial equipment covers, often utilize polyester thread. Its durability and ability to withstand high stress make it an ideal choice for these applications.

✓ *Linen Thread*

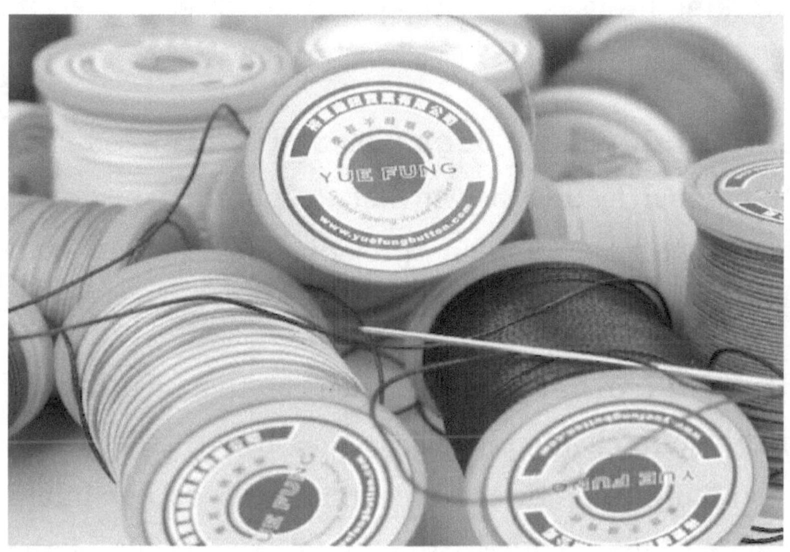

Linen thread is a natural thread option ***made from flax fibers***. It is highly regarded for its strength, durability, and unique aesthetic appeal. It offers a rustic and vintage look to your stitches, adding character and authenticity to your leather pieces.

The linen thread is strong and provides excellent resistance to wear and tear. It is also available in different thicknesses, allowing you to choose the right thread size for your project. While linen thread may not have the color variety of synthetic threads, it offers a natural and timeless elegance that complements certain leather items and crafting styles.

Linen thread is commonly used in traditional or historical leatherworking projects, as it replicates the threads used in the past, such as:

1. ***Traditional leather bags***: Linen thread is often used in traditional leather bag making, replicating historical stitching techniques and providing a vintage and authentic look to the stitches.

2. ***Historical leather goods***: When creating historical or period-inspired leather goods, such as armor, accessories, or costuming, linen thread is commonly used to maintain authenticity and replicate the stitching methods of the era.

3. ***Leathercraft with a vintage or historical aesthetic***: For leather projects that aim to achieve a vintage or historical look, such as antique-style journals or retro-inspired accessories, linen thread is a popular choice to enhance the overall appearance.

✓ *Cotton Thread*

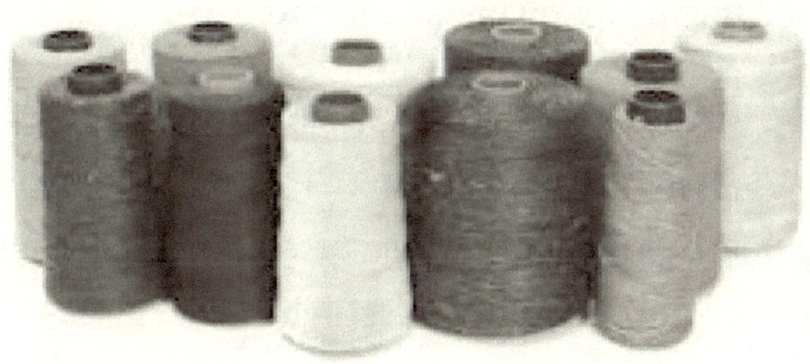

Cotton thread is ***a natural thread option*** known for its softness and versatility. It is a more delicate thread than synthetic options but can still be suitable for specific leather projects. Cotton thread is available in a wide range of colors, including neutral colors such as white and bold colors such as red, allowing you to add visual interest and decorative touches to your leather pieces. Cotton thread offers a softer and more subtle look to your stitches, providing a gentle contrast against the ruggedness of leather. However, it's important to note that ***cotton thread may not be as durable as synthetic threads*** and may not withstand heavy use or stress.

Cotton thread is commonly used for lightweight leather items or decorative stitching, where strength requirements are not as high.

It is widely used for the following leather items:

1. ***Garments made from lightweight leather***: Cotton thread is suitable for stitching lightweight leather garments, such as jackets, vests, or skirts, providing a softer and more subtle look to the stitches.

2. ***Decorative stitching on leather accessories***: When adding decorative details or embellishments to leather accessories like bags, wallets, or keychains, cotton thread offers a delicate and decorative touch.

3. Delicate leather projects: For delicate leather projects requiring more delicate stitches, such as small leather crafts or intricate leather jewelry, cotton thread is preferred due to its softness and finer appearance.

When choosing the right thread for your leather projects, consider the specific requirements of your project, such as the intended use, expected stress or tension on the stitches, and desired aesthetic appeal.

Evaluate each thread type's strength, durability, and compatibility with your project needs. Consider factors like UV resistance, water resistance, color availability, and the desired visual effect. By considering these factors and understanding the characteristics of each thread type, you can make an informed decision that ensures the longevity and visual appeal of your leather pieces.

Marking and Measuring Tools

- **Leather Marking Pen**

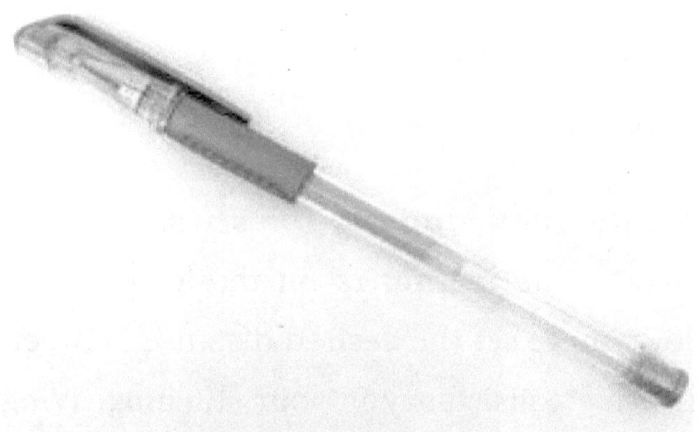

This pen is specially ***designed for marking stitching lines, patterns, or measurements on the leather.*** The ink is formulated to create precise and visible marks that can easily be wiped off or disappear with time. The fine tip allows for accuracy and ensures the marks don't bleed or smudge on the leather surface.

- **Wing Divider**

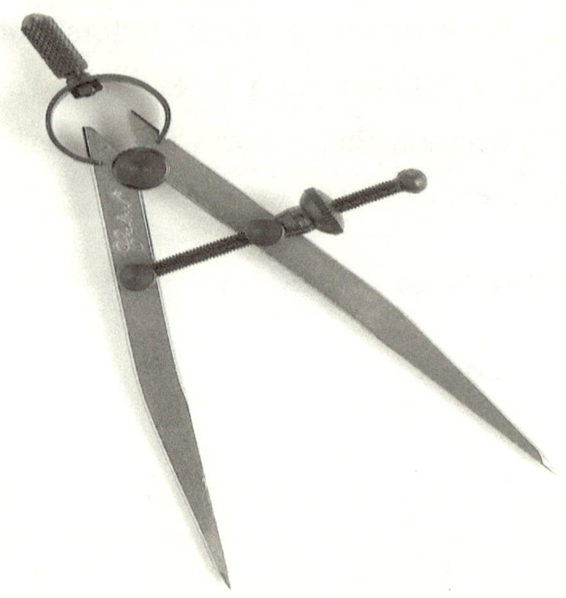

This tool ***helps create even spacing for stitching and marking accurate measurements*** on the leather. The adjustable legs allow you to set the desired distance between marks or lines, ensuring consistency in your stitching. Wing dividers are particularly useful when marking multiple parallel lines or dividing leather.

- **Ruler or Tape Measure**

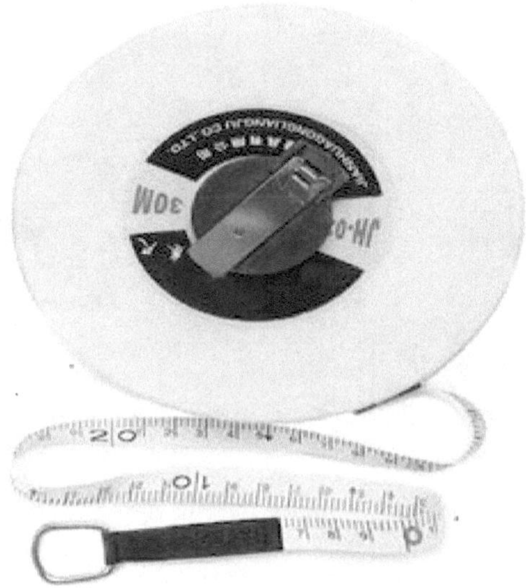

Tape Measure 1

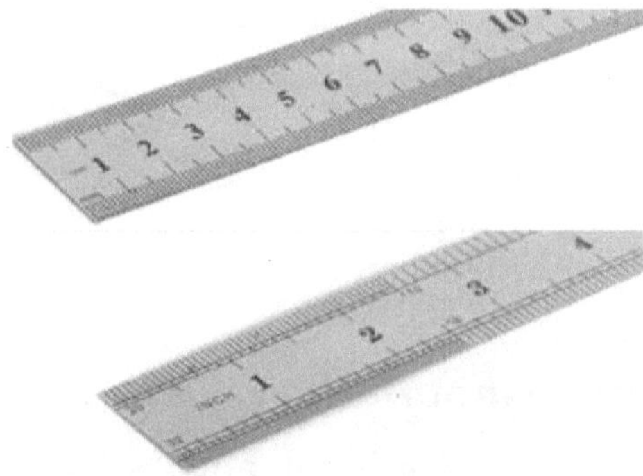

Ruler 1

These are essential tools for ***measuring and marking dimensions accurately*** on the leather. They help ensure precision when cutting patterns, determining stitch lines, or measuring specific areas of your project.

A transparent ruler or a flexible tape measure allows for easy reading and provides flexibility when working with irregularly shaped pieces.

Edge Finishing Tools

- **Edge Beveler**

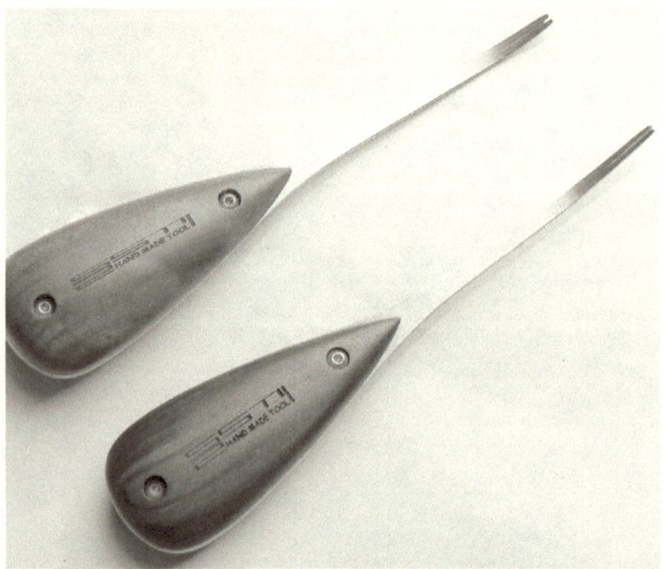

This tool is ***used to round and smooth the edges of cut leather pieces***, giving them a professional and polished appearance. The beveler's curved blade removes sharp corners and creates a slightly beveled edge. This not only enhances the aesthetics of the leather but also helps prevent premature wear and fraying.

Beveling the edges also allows for smoother edge dyeing or burnishing, resulting in a clean and finished look.

- **Edge Slicker**

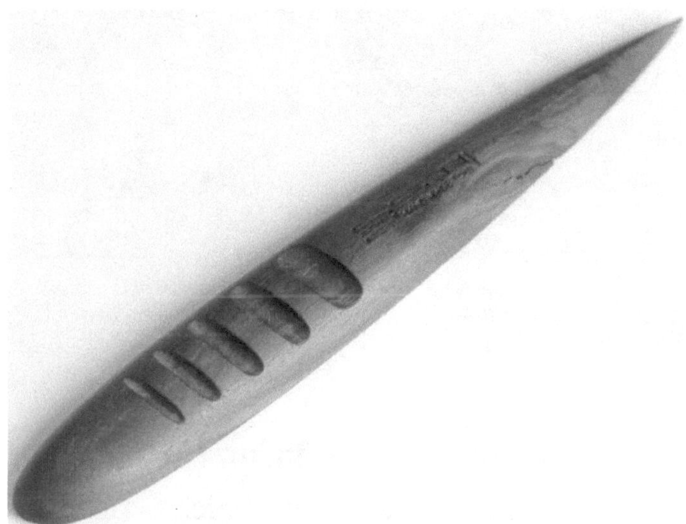

This tool is ***used for burnishing and polishing* the edges of the leather**. Rubbing the slicker along the leather edge generates heat that helps seal and smoothen the fibers. This process compresses the fibers, making them more resistant to fraying and creating a glossy and professional-looking edge. For various personal preferences, edge slickers are available in different shapes and materials, such as wood, bone, or plastic.

- **Sandpaper**

This tool is ***used for sanding and refining the edges of the leather***, mainly when working with thicker or more rigid leather. Sandpaper helps remove roughness, unevenness, or imperfections from the edges, resulting in a smooth and clean finish.

Starting with coarser grits and progressing to finer ones allows for gradual refinement and ensures a polished edge ready for further finishing techniques.

These tools form the foundation of a well-equipped leatherworking toolkit. As you delve deeper into the craft, you may discover additional specialized tools that cater to specific techniques or projects. Investing in quality tools enhances your leatherworking experience and improves your leather creations' overall quality and longevity.

Please note that the above descriptions provide a general overview of each tool. Each tool has unique features, variations, and techniques for optimal use. Exploring and experimenting with different tools will help you refine your skills and find the tools that suit your personal style and project.

Next, we will learn how to create a functional leatherworking workspace.

Chapter 3: Setting Up Your Leatherworking Workspace

Creating a well-designed workspace is crucial for optimal productivity, creativity, and overall enjoyment of the leatherworking process. This chapter will explore the importance of a thoughtfully designed workspace and discuss critical considerations when choosing the location.

We will delve into designing the layout, including work surfaces, tool organization, and ergonomic considerations. Additionally, we will explore lighting and storage solutions and the importance of safety measures. Finally, we will discuss on drawbacks of neglecting to choose a suitable workspace.

Importance of a Well-Designed Leatherworking Workspace

Creating a well-designed workspace for your leatherworking endeavors offers numerous benefits that greatly enhance your overall experience and productivity.

Here are some key reasons why a thoughtfully designed workspace is essential:

- **Enhanced Focus and Concentration**

A well-designed leatherworking workspace provides a dedicated and focused environment to immerse yourself in your craft fully. By separating your workspace from other activities, such as household chores or personal distractions, you can create a space dedicated to your leatherworking projects.

This separation helps minimize external disturbances and allows you to concentrate on your work, resulting in improved focus and increased attention to detail. You can fully engage in the creative process and achieve higher craftsmanship with fewer distractions.

- **Increased Efficiency and Organization**

Efficiency and organization are crucial elements in any workspace. A well-designed leatherworking space promotes efficient workflow and streamlines your processes. By organizing your tools, materials, and equipment in a logical and accessible manner, you can eliminate unnecessary time spent searching for items and reduce frustration. Having designated storage areas, such as tool racks, shelves, and drawers, ensures that everything has a place, making it easier to locate and retrieve what you need quickly.

An organized workspace also allows smoother transitions between tasks and helps you stay focused and on track, ultimately improving productivity.

- **Optimal Ergonomics**

Ergonomics is an essential consideration in any workspace, including leatherworking. A well-designed setup considers proper workbench height, chair ergonomics, and tool placement. Ergonomics focuses on creating a workspace that supports your body's natural alignment and minimizes the risk of strain or injury.

For example, ensuring that your workbench is at the correct height reduces the strain on your back and shoulders, while a comfortable and supportive chair promotes good posture. Proper tool placement ensures that your most frequently used tools are within easy reach, minimizing the need for excessive reaching or stretching.

By optimizing the ergonomics of your leatherworking workspace, you can work comfortably for more extended periods and reduce the risk of physical discomfort or injuries.

- **Safety and Risk Management**

A dedicated leatherworking workspace allows you to establish safety measures specific to your craft. ***Safety should always be a priority*** when working with tools, chemicals, and potentially hazardous materials. By designing your workspace with safety in mind, you can mitigate potential risks and create a secure working environment.

For example, proper ventilation systems can be installed to remove fumes from adhesives, dyes, or solvents, protecting your respiratory health. Adequate lighting ensures clear visibility, reducing the likelihood of accidents or mistakes. You can also designate separate areas for activities such as tool sharpening or leather conditioning to minimize the risk of cross-contamination or accidents.

By implementing safety measures, you create a workspace that promotes security/safety, allowing you to focus on your craft with peace of mind.

- **Creative Inspiration and Motivation**

A well-designed leatherworking workspace can serve as a source of creative inspiration and motivation. Personalizing your space with elements that reflect your style, interests, and achievements can ignite your creativity and make your workspace an inviting and inspiring workplace. Displaying finished projects, incorporating artwork or photographs that inspire you, or arranging tools and materials aesthetically pleasingly can enhance your pride and motivation. Creating a visually appealing and personalized space can stimulate your imagination, fuel your passion for leatherworking, and constantly remind you of your creative potential.

Indeed, a well-designed leatherworking workspace is essential for maximizing your focus, productivity, creativity, and safety. You can optimize your working environment to support your craft and enhance your overall leatherworking experience by creating a dedicated, organized space that considers ergonomics and personalization. A thoughtfully designed workspace improves efficiency and functionality and creates a space to fully immerse yourself in your art, fostering a sense of inspiration and motivation.

Designing Your Leatherworking Workspace

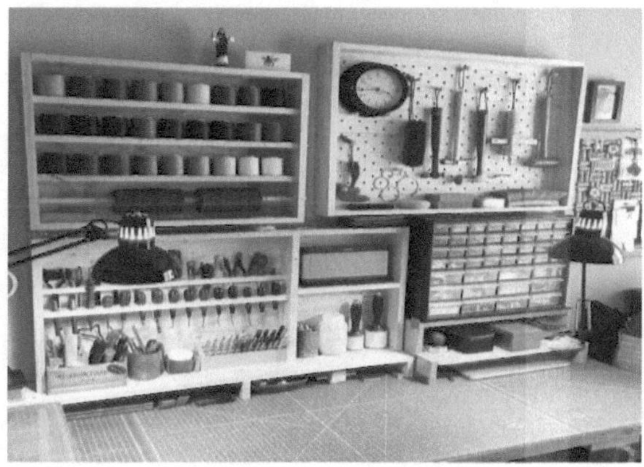

Workspace

Here we'll cover everything you need to know to create a space that fosters your passion for leatherworking. Let's embark on this exciting journey and build a workspace that elevates your craft to new heights!

- **Selecting the Right Location**

Selecting the right location for your leatherworking workspace is crucial for creating a conducive environment that fosters creativity, productivity, and comfort. The location you choose ***should align with your workflow, practical needs, and personal preferences***.

Here are some factors to consider when selecting the right location for your leatherworking workspace:

- ✓ ***Space Availability:*** Assess the available space in your home or workspace. Choose a location that offers enough room for your workbench, storage solutions, and any additional furniture or equipment you may need. Avoid areas that are too cramped, as they can hinder your movement and productivity.
- ✓ ***Accessibility*:** Consider the accessibility of the location. Ideally, your leatherworking workspace should be easily accessible from other areas in your home or workplace. Being close to the main entrance, restroom, or kitchen can be convenient, especially if you spend long hours in your workspace.
- ✓ ***Privacy*:** Depending on your personal preference and working style, consider privacy as a factor. Some leatherworkers prefer a secluded area where they can focus without distractions, while others enjoy working in a more open or communal setting.
- ✓ ***Inspiration and Motivation*:** Consider a location that inspires and motivates you by surrounding yourself with elements that resonate with your craft, such as artwork,

leatherworking samples or items that reflect your creative vision.

✓ ***Future Growth*:** Consider your future growth as a leatherworker. If you anticipate expanding your workspace or investing in additional equipment, choose a location that can accommodate these changes without causing disruptions to your workflow.

- **Choosing the Perfect Workbench**

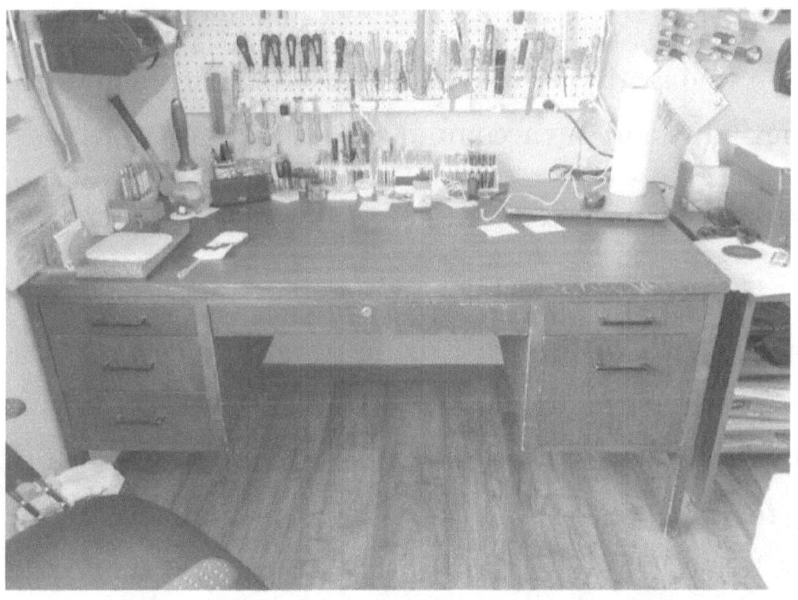

A workbench is the heart of any leatherworking workspace, and selecting the right one is crucial for maximizing productivity, comfort, and craftsmanship.

Here are some key considerations to keep in mind when choosing the perfect workbench:

✓ ***Size and Surface Area***

Begin by assessing the available space in your workshop or designated leatherworking area. Choose a workbench that fits comfortably within this space without making it feel cramped.

Ensure the bench is large enough to provide sufficient surface area for cutting, stitching, assembling, and other tasks you frequently perform. A larger workbench allows for more flexibility and can accommodate larger leather pieces.

✓ ***Sturdiness and Stability***

A sturdy and stable workbench is essential for precision work and safety. Look for a bench made from durable materials like solid wood or metal. Consider the weight-bearing capacity of the bench, as some leatherworking tasks, such as cutting or hammering, may exert significant force on the surface. Avoid lightweight or wobbly workbenches that could compromise the quality of your work.

✓ *Height and Ergonomics*

Proper ergonomics are critical for maintaining comfort and preventing fatigue during long hours of crafting. Look for a workbench height that allows you to comfortably work while standing or sitting on a suitable stool or chair. Many leatherworkers prefer an ***adjustable workbench***, enabling them to customize the height to their individual needs.

Here are some guidelines to help you determine the appropriate workbench height:

1. **Neutral Posture**: When standing at your workbench, aim for a neutral posture with your shoulders relaxed and your arms comfortably bent at a 90-degree angle. This position allows you to work efficiently without straining your muscles or joints.
2. **Elbow Height**: Measure the height from the floor to your elbows when standing in a relaxed posture. Your workbench height should align with this measurement to provide optimal support and prevent strain on your upper body.
3. **Seated Height:** If you prefer working while sitting, the workbench height should be adjustable to accommodate your seated position comfortably. When seated, your feet

should rest flat on the floor, and your thighs should parallel the ground.

4. **Trial and Error:** Experiment with different workbench heights to find the most comfortable and ergonomic position for you. Depending on their height and personal preferences, some individuals may prefer a slightly higher or lower workbench.

5. **Tool Accessibility**: Consider the height of your tools and materials when choosing the workbench height. Your tools should be easily accessible without causing you to strain or bend awkwardly while working.

6. **Customizability:** Opt for an adjustable workbench that lets you fine-tune the height according to your needs. This flexibility ensures you can adapt the workbench to different projects and working positions.

7. **Anti-Fatigue Mats**: If you prefer to stand while working, consider using anti-fatigue mats in front of your workbench. These mats provide cushioning and support for your feet, reducing fatigue during prolonged crafting sessions.

8. **Personal Comfort:** The right workbench height should be comfortable and support your needs. Trust your body's feedback and adjust until you find the ideal height for your leatherworking endeavors.

✓ ***Budget and Quality***

Set a budget for your workbench but be willing to invest in a high-quality product that will endure heavy use over time. A solidly built workbench may cost more initially but will pay off with increased longevity and performance.

- **Organizing Your Tools and Materials**

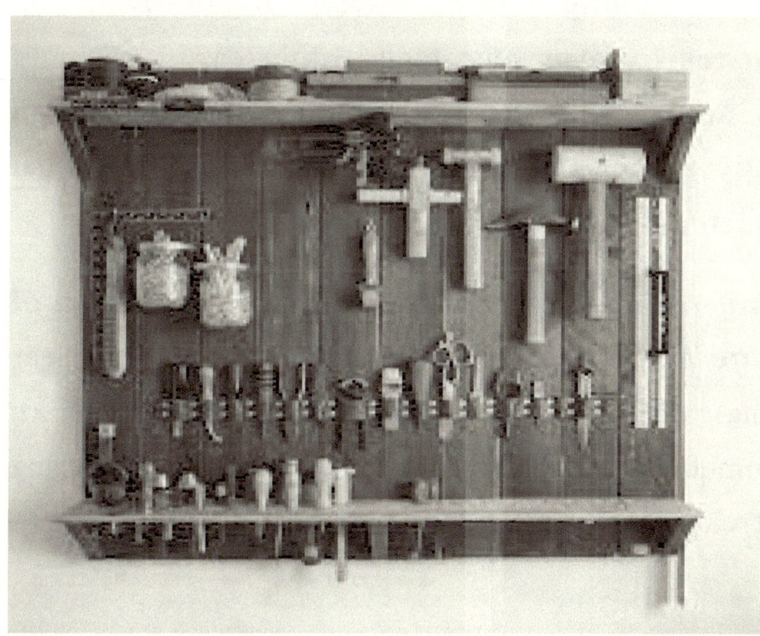

An organized tool setup is a game-changer for any leatherworker. Having a designated area to store your tools not only saves time but also keeps your workspace clutter-free and enhances your overall efficiency.

So, how do you organize your tools and materials?

- ✓ ***Begin by categorizing your tools based on their functions***. Group cutting tools together, stitching tools together, and so on. This categorization makes it easier to find the right tool when you need it, preventing unnecessary searches and interruptions in your workflow.
- ✓ ***Consider using tool racks, pegboards, or toolboxes*** to keep your tools within easy reach and neatly arranged. As for wall-mounted racks, they can display your tools beautifully while also serving as a visual reminder of the tools at your disposal.
- ✓ ***Adding labels or color-coding to your tool storage*** can further enhance organization. With clear labeling, you can quickly identify tools, even if they are not immediately visible, saving you time and effort during your creative process.

- **Prioritizing Safety Measures**

Safety is paramount in any workspace, and a leatherworking workshop is no exception. Working with various tools, chemicals, and materials requires caution to avoid accidents and injuries, such as:

✓ Always keep a well-stocked first aid kit readily available in your workspace. In the event of minor injuries, having immediate access to bandages, antiseptic wipes, and pain relief medication can make a significant difference.

✓ Familiarize yourself with the safety guidelines and precautions for each tool and equipment you use. Read the user manuals and follow manufacturer recommendations to use your tools safely and effectively.

✓ Whenever you are working with adhesives, dyes, or finishing products, ensure adequate ventilation in your workspace. Proper ventilation helps dissipate fumes and prevents the buildup of harmful vapors. If necessary, consider using a fume extractor or working in a well-ventilated area.

✓ Invest in safety equipment like protective gloves and goggles and use them when handling chemicals or performing tasks that pose a risk of injury. Prioritize your safety and the safety of those around you to enjoy your leatherworking journey without incidents.

- **Ensuring Adequate Ventilation**

Ensuring adequate ventilation is crucial in your leatherworking workshop to maintain a healthy and safe environment.

Here are some tips to ensure sufficient ventilation in your workspace:

✓ ***Natural Ventilation*:** If possible, position your workspace near a window or any openings that allow fresh air to flow into the area. Natural ventilation helps in circulating air and dispersing any fumes that might be generated during the leatherworking process.

✓ ***Use Fans or Exhaust Systems*:** Install fans or exhaust systems in your workspace to improve air circulation and draw out fumes. Ventilation fans can be placed near workstations to direct fumes away from your breathing zone. Exhaust systems are particularly beneficial if you're using adhesives, dyes, or other materials that emit strong odors or fumes.

- ✓ ***Ventilate Workstation for Specific Tasks***: For tasks that involve using strong chemicals or glues, work in a designated area with enhanced ventilation. If possible, set up this area near an exhaust fan or open window to help disperse the fumes quickly.

- ✓ ***Personal Protective Equipment (PPE)*****:** Wear appropriate personal protective equipment, such as respiratory masks or respirators, when working with materials that generate significant fumes or dust. PPE helps to protect your respiratory system from exposure to harmful substances.

- **Designating a Cutting Area**

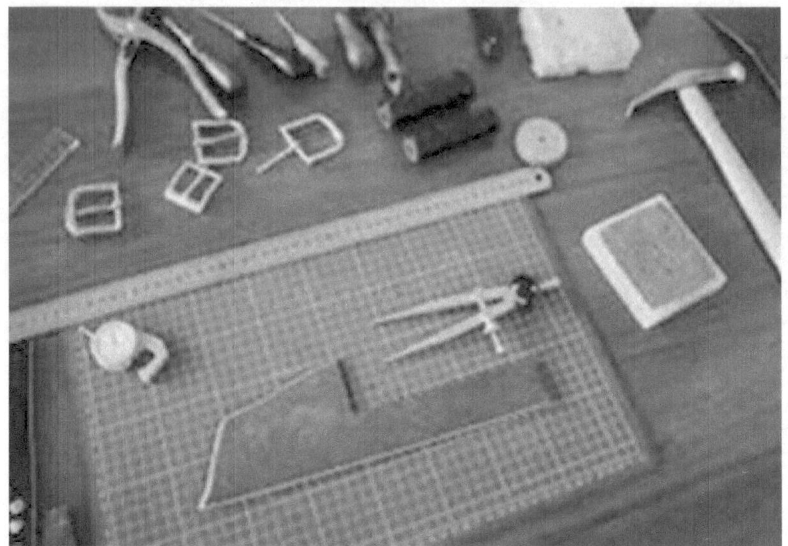

Designating a cutting area is a vital step in designing your leatherworking workshop. This specialized space is where you'll perform precision cutting and trimming tasks, ensuring the quality and accuracy of your leather pieces.

Here's some ways of creating an efficient and safe cutting area:

✓ ***Cutting Mat***

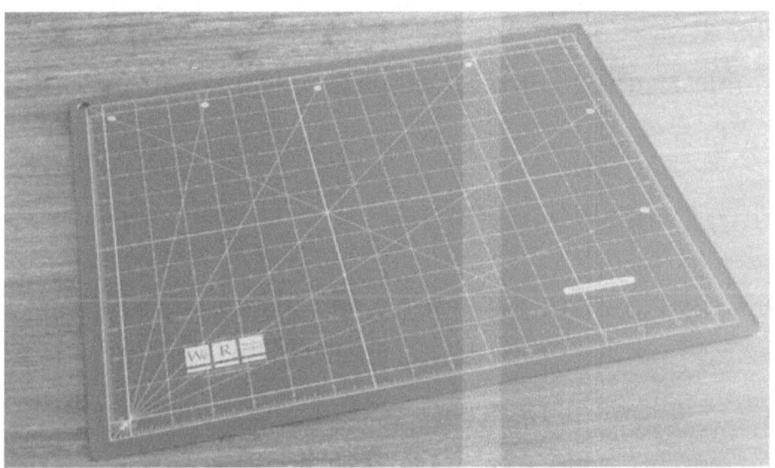

Place a high-quality self-healing cutting mat on your workbench or a dedicated cutting table. This protective surface not only preserves your workbench but also extends the lifespan of your cutting tools, such as rotary cutters and utility knives.

✓ ***Clear Work Space***

Ensure to keep the area around the cutting mat clear of any clutter or unnecessary items. A clutter-free space ensures smooth movement and minimizes the risk of accidents while cutting.

✓ ***Proper Lighting***

Ensure adequate lighting over the cutting area to see the details clearly and make precise cuts. You can use task lights or adjustable lamps to direct focused illumination onto the cutting surface.

✓ ***Cutting Tools Accessibility***

Store your cutting tools, such as rotary cutters, utility knives, and scissors, in a designated area near the cutting mat. This arrangement allows easy access to the tools you frequently use during cutting tasks.

- **Work in Progress (WIP) Storage**

Work-in-progress (WIP) storage is a crucial consideration in your leatherworking workspace. Proper storage solutions for your ongoing projects ensure that your workspace remains organized, efficient, and minimizes the risk of damage to your work.

Here are some factors to consider when setting up work-in-progress storage:

- ✓ ***Temporary Storage Solutions*:** For your ongoing projects, consider using temporary storage solutions like bins, trays, or shelves, depending on the size and nature of your leatherworking projects. These can hold partially completed pieces, cut leather parts, or other materials related to your ongoing projects. Temporary storage keeps your workspace tidy and prevents confusion between different projects.

- ✓ ***Project-Specific Containers*:** For larger or more complex projects, consider using project-specific containers or bins. Ensure to label these containers with the name or description of the project to easily identify and access the necessary materials and tools for each project. This approach helps you quickly pick up where you left off when returning to a project.

- ✓ ***Project Tracking***: Use a project tracking system, such as a project journal or digital notes, to keep track of your ongoing projects. Ensure to note down the current status, materials used, changes made, and any challenges encountered. This documentation helps you pick up from the place or step you left off and provides valuable insights for future projects.

Choosing Comfortable Seating

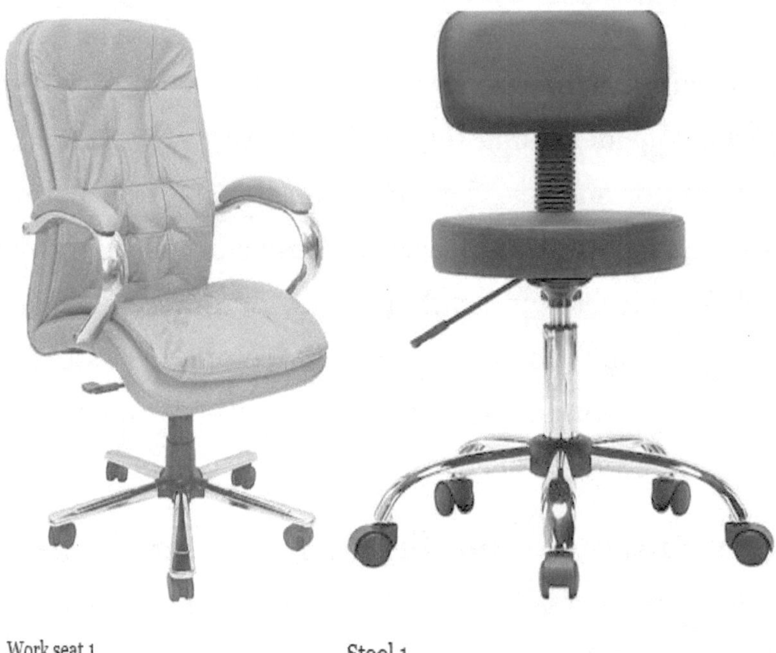

Work seat 1 Stool 1

Choosing comfortable seating is essential for maintaining good posture and preventing fatigue during long leatherworking sessions.

Here's how to select comfortable seating for your leatherworking workshop:

✓ ***Ergonomic Chairs or Stools*:** Invest in an ergonomic chair or stool that provides proper lumbar support and encourages good posture. Look for chairs with adjustable height and backrests, allowing you to customize the seating position to your specific needs.

- ✓ ***Consider Cushioning*:** Opt for seating with adequate cushioning to provide comfort during long hours of sitting. The padding should be firm enough to support your weight while offering enough softness to prevent discomfort.

- ✓ ***Footrests:*** If you choose a stool, consider one with a footrest or a foot ring. A footrest provides support and helps improve circulation in your legs, reducing fatigue and discomfort.

- ✓ ***Test Before Purchasing*:** If possible, try out different seating options before making a decision. Sit on the chairs or stools for an extended period to assess their comfort and support.

- **Keeping Cleaning Supplies Handy**

Keeping cleaning supplies handy is an essential aspect of maintaining a tidy and organized leatherworking workspace.

Here are some tips for keeping cleaning supplies easily accessible in your leatherworking workspace:

✓ ***Cleaning Station***

Designate a specific area or corner of your workspace as a cleaning station. This area should have all the necessary cleaning supplies neatly organized and within arm's reach.

Consider using a small table, cart, or shelving unit to keep the cleaning tools and materials well-arranged.

✓ ***Cleaning Schedule***

Create a cleaning schedule to ensure regular maintenance of your workspace. Dedicate specific times for cleaning, either at the end of each workday or before starting a new project. Consistency in cleaning keeps your workspace organized and ready for crafting.

✓ ***Clean as You Go***

Incorporate a "clean as you go" approach during your leatherworking process. Whenever, you finish a task, take a moment to clean up any debris or spills before moving on to the next step. This practice prevents messes from accumulating and makes the final cleanup more manageable.

✓ ***Encourage Cleanliness***

Suppose you share your workspace with others; in that case, encourage everyone to maintain cleanliness and respect the designated cleaning station. Keeping the area tidy is a collective responsibility that ensures a pleasant and efficient working environment for all.

Drawbacks of Neglecting to Choose the Right Workspace for Leatherworking

Not choosing the suitable workshop for leatherworking can have several disadvantages that may negatively impact your overall crafting experience and progress as a leatherworker.

Here are some of the drawbacks of not selecting the appropriate workspace:

- **Safety Hazards**

A poorly designed workspace can lead to safety hazards and accidents. Inadequate storage and organization of tools and materials may increase the risk of injuries from sharp tools, chemical exposure, or tripping hazards.

- **Inefficiency**

A disorganized and cluttered workspace can lead to inefficiency and frustration. Difficulty finding tools or materials can waste valuable time, hinder workflow, and impede your progress on projects.

- **Demotivation**

A poorly designed workspace is likely demotivating and make you less inclined to spend time on your leatherworking hobby or passion. Lack of motivation may hinder your progress and prevent you from reaching your full potential as a leatherworker.

- **Potential Health Risks**

Inadequate ventilation or failure to address fumes from adhesives or chemicals may pose health risks. Prolonged exposure to harmful fumes in a poorly ventilated space can lead to respiratory issues and other health concerns.

The workspace you choose for your leatherworking endeavors plays a significant role in your success and growth as a leather artisan. Taking the time to design a suitable workspace that addresses your needs, fosters creativity, and prioritizes safety is an investment that can elevate your leatherworking experience and lead to greater fulfillment and achievement in the craft. Neglecting to create such a workspace can result in drawbacks like reduced productivity and compromised safety. Therefore, strive to craft an inspiring and well-equipped leatherworking environment to unlock your full potential and enjoy the journey of creating beautiful leather pieces.

Section 2: Mastering the Leatherworking Process

In this chapter, we will explore the various steps involved in the leatherworking process so you can master each step in bringing your idea to life.

In the first step, we will dive into cutting, where we will begin by mastering precision cuts with various tools suitable for different leather thicknesses. You will learn to overcome challenges like cutting thin leather without distortion and discover multiple cutting techniques like straight and curved cuts.

The second step takes us to leather stamping; you will discover how to emboss intricate designs onto leather surfaces to create unique and artistic patterns. Explore the stamping process step-by-step, from choosing the correct stamps to achieving consistent impressions.

In the third step, we explore leather tooling, where we'll learn to add depth and character to leather creations through beautifully embossed designs. Delve into different tooling techniques like floral tooling and backgrounding, and overcome challenges such as tool placement and achieving consistent depths.

Our journey in the fourth step leads us to leather dyeing and finishing, exploring different dye types and techniques to add color and professional touch to our leather projects. Discover the art of edge finishing, mastering methods like burnishing and edge painting to achieve polished and refined edges.

By embracing each step of the leatherworking process, you unlock your creative potential and craft impressive leather pieces that reflect your passion and dedication to this timeless craft. With patience and practice, you'll gain the confidence to embark on more ambitious projects and infuse your work with your unique style and flair.

So, let's embark on this enriching journey together, mastering the art of leatherworking and bringing your leatherworking ideas to life.

Chapter 4: Step 1: Leather Cutting

Why You Should Learn Leather Cutting

Cutting is a crucial step in leatherworking whose mastery will ensure:

- **You don't waste material**; you'll find that you can create leather pieces with precision and efficiency, minimizing material wastage and making the most out of every inch of leather. This saves costs and allows you to embark on more ambitious projects without worrying about running out of material.
- **You achieve cleaner and neater edges**, producing a more professional and polished look for your leather projects. It sets the foundation for successful stitching and assembling, ensuring that your finished piece has a cohesive and well-crafted appearance.
- **Efficiency and productivity** as you work on multiple pieces or bulk production. With confidence in your cutting skills, you can easily tackle complex patterns and large-scale projects, knowing you can consistently achieve the desired shapes and dimensions.

- **It opens up a world of possibilities** in your leatherworking journey. Leather cutting is a foundational skill that lays the groundwork for your success as you progress to explore other techniques and create unique and beautifully crafted leather pieces.

So, let's delve into the art of precision cutting, learning the right tools and methods to elevate your leatherworking experience to new heights.

Different projects will call for different cutting techniques, which include:

Straight Cuts

A straight cut involves using a sharp cutting tool, such as a leather cutting knife or rotary cutter, to make a precise and even cut along a straight line on the leather surface. This type of cut is relatively simple but requires accuracy and control to achieve clean and professional-looking results.

Let's delve deeper into its significance and when it becomes essential:

- **Applications and Importance of Straight Cuts**

✓ ***Precision and Clean Edges:*** One of the primary reasons to use a straight cut is to achieve precise and clean edges on the leather. This technique allows you to maintain straight lines without deviations or jagged edges, resulting in a polished and professional look for your leather pieces. Whether you're creating a sleek leather belt, a minimalist wallet, or a structured leather bag, straight cuts provide the foundational elements for a well-crafted and visually appealing product.

- ✓ ***Symmetry and Consistency:*** A straight cut is vital when working on projects that demand symmetry and consistency, such as leather panels for bags or covers for books and journals. Following a straight path ensures that each piece matches its counterpart accurately, achieving a harmonious and balanced final product. Consistent edges also facilitate smooth assembly and stitching, streamlining the construction process.

- ✓ ***Refining and Trimming***: Straight cuts are frequently employed in the final stages of leatherworking to trim and refine the edges of completed projects. Whether it's a leather bag, a clutch, or a key holder, using a straight cut to trim excess leather provides a clean finish, removing any uneven or unwanted sections. This finishing touch enhances the overall presentation of your leather creations, making them stand out with professional finesse.

- ✓ ***Combining Leather Pieces***: Combining different leather pieces is common in specific leatherworking techniques, like patchwork or mosaic designs. And to achieve a seamless and cohesive composition, precision straight cuts are essential. Whether you're creating a stunning leather art piece or a unique leather accent for a larger project, accurate straight cuts ensure that the pieces fit together flawlessly.

- ✓ ***Versatility and Adaptability***: Straight cuts are incredibly versatile and can be applied across various leatherworking projects. This cutting technique is utilized throughout crafting, from small accessories like keychains and coin pouches to larger items like briefcases or messenger bags. Whether you're a beginner or a seasoned leatherworker, mastering the art of straight cuts will serve you well in numerous creative endeavors.

- **Challenges You May Face in Straight Cuts During Leatherworking**

They include:

1. ***Inaccuracy***

For beginners, achieving precise measurements and straight lines is likely challenging. Even a slight deviation from the intended line can lead to uneven cuts and affect the overall appearance of the leather piece.

Overcoming Inaccuracy:

✓ ***Use Measuring Tools***: Always use a ruler, measuring tape, or leather marking pen to mark the desired length or shape on the leather before cutting. Measuring and marking accurately will provide a clear guide for the cutting process.

✓ ***Take Your Time***: Avoid rushing the cutting process. Take time to properly align the cutting tool with the marked line and proceed with controlled and steady movements. Precision comes with patience.

✓ ***Straight Edge or Cutting Guide***: For longer cuts or straight lines, use a straight edge or cutting guide to maintain a straight path. This technique will help you avoid unintentional deviations and ensure clean cuts.

2. *Cutting Tool Slippage*

When using a sharp cutting tool, such as a leather cutting knife or rotary cutter in straight cuts, there is a risk of the tool slipping on the leather surface. This risk can result in jagged edges or accidental cuts in unintended areas. Overcoming cutting tool slippage is crucial to ensure safety and accuracy in leather cutting.

Here are some strategies to prevent and overcome cutting tool slippage:

- ✓ ***Use a Proper Cutting Surface***: Place the leather on a suitable cutting surface, such as a self-healing cutting mat or a sturdy workbench. Doing this will provide a stable and non-slippery surface for your cutting tool.
- ✓ ***Check Cutting Tool Condition***: Ensure that your cutting tool, whether a leather cutting knife or a rotary cutter, is in good condition. Replace blades as needed to maintain sharpness and efficiency.
- ✓ ***Use Appropriate Cutting Angle***: Hold the cutting tool at the appropriate angle to the leather surface. For straight cuts, keep the blade perpendicular to the leather. For curved cuts, adjust the angle to match the curve smoothly.

- ✓ ***Secure the Leather***: Hold the leather firmly in place with your non-dominant hand while cutting. Doing this prevents unnecessary movement and minimizes the chances of the cutting tool slipping.

- ✓ ***Avoid Excessive Force***: Apply even and controlled pressure on the cutting tool, avoiding excessive force that can cause the tool to skip or slip. Let the sharpness of the blade do the work rather than forcing it through the leather.

- ✓ ***Practice and Technique***: Practice cutting techniques on scrap leather to improve your skills and gain better control over the cutting tool. Proper technique, including steady hand movements and consistent pressure, will reduce the likelihood of slippage.

- ✓ ***Maintain a Safe Grip***: Hold the cutting tool securely, ensuring it fits comfortably in your hand. Some cutting tools come with ergonomic handles that provide better control and reduce hand fatigue.

- ✓ ***Cut in Well-lit Area***: Ensure sufficient lighting in your workspace to see the cutting lines clearly. A well-lit area reduces the chances of making inaccurate cuts and minimizes the need to redo cuts.

- ✓ ***Check Cutting Direction***: Double-check the direction of your cutting line before cutting. Verify that the tool is appropriately aligned and positioned before proceeding.
- ✓ ***Be Mindful of Blade Depth***: If using a rotary cutter with adjustable blade depth, ensure the blade is set to the appropriate depth for your specific leather thickness. Doing this prevents the blade from cutting too deeply and causing unintended slipping.

3. *Straightness*

Maintaining a straight cutting line throughout the entire length of the leather piece can be difficult, especially when cutting longer pieces. Inconsistent straightness can affect a project's fitting and assembly of leather components.

Here is how you can overcome difficulty in maintaining straightness:

- ✓ ***Straight Edge or Ruler as a Guide***: Use a straight edge or ruler to maintain straightness in longer cuts. This will help you achieve clean and precise lines.
- ✓ ***Steady Hand Movements***: Keep your hand steady and avoid sudden movements while cutting. Slow, continuous motions along the marked line will improve the straightness of the cut.

4. *Wastage*

Straight-cutting mistakes can lead to material wastage, as leather is not easily reversible or repairable once cut. Efficiently utilizing the leather and minimizing wastage is essential, especially when working with expensive or limited materials.

Here is how you can overcome wastage in leather cutting:

- ✓ ***Plan your cuts***: Before starting, carefully plan the layout of your pattern on the leather to optimize the use of the material and minimize wastage.
- ✓ ***Measure accurately***: Take precise measurements and mark your cutting lines carefully to avoid mistakes that could lead to excess waste.
- ✓ ***Use templates***: Utilize templates or stencils to trace and cut consistent shapes, ensuring you avoid unnecessary mistakes and maximize leather usage.
- ✓ ***Practice cutting techniques***: Improve your cutting skills through practice on scrap leather, gaining confidence and reducing the likelihood of mistakes on your main project.

✓ ***Optimize positioning***: Arrange your leather pieces strategically on the cutting surface, leaving as little space as possible between them to reduce scrap.

✓ ***Save smaller scraps***: Keep smaller leftover pieces as they might come in handy for future projects, repairs, or smaller accessories.

✓ ***Invest in nesting software***: Nesting software is a specialized computer program used in manufacturing and production industries, including leatherworking. Use nesting software that automatically arranges pieces for bulk production or complex patterns to minimize wastage.

One example of nesting software commonly used in the leather industry is ***"OptiTex Nest++."*** [1]This software is designed to optimize the layout and placement of leather patterns on the cutting surface, minimizing waste and maximizing material utilization. It helps manufacturers and designers efficiently plan and organize their leather-cutting processes, saving time and resources.

---

1 https://www.optitex.com/nesting-software/↩

Here's how it works:

- **Pattern Input**: Provide the software with the digital patterns of the leather pieces they want to cut. You can import the patterns from design software or create them within the nesting software.
- **Material Information**: Input information about the size and dimensions of the leather material you are using, such as the length, width, and quantity of the leather sheets available for cutting.
- **Optimization Algorithm:** The nesting software employs advanced optimization algorithms to arrange the digital patterns efficiently on the given leather sheets. It analyzes the shapes and sizes of the patterns and calculates the most optimal arrangement to minimize material wastage.
- **Nesting Layout**: The software then generates a nesting layout, visually representing how the digital patterns will be placed on the leather sheets. It shows how each piece will be cut and arranged to utilize the leather material to its fullest potential.
- **Cutting Instructions**: The nesting software provides instructions you can use with automated cutting machines or manual cutting processes. These

instructions guide the cutting process, indicating where to cut and how to position the leather pieces for maximum efficiency.

- ✓ ***Evaluate the layout***: Before cutting, double-check the layout to ensure you've utilized the leather efficiently and made the most of the available space.

- ✓ ***Consider alternative uses***: If you have unavoidable waste, explore creative ways to repurpose or recycle the leftover leather for smaller projects or decorative elements.

These strategies can significantly reduce wastage and make the most of your leather materials during cutting.

5. *Handling Large Pieces*

Handling large leather pieces in straight cuts is potentially challenging due to their size and weight.

To overcome this challenge, consider the following strategies:

- ✓ ***Prepare Your Workspace***: Ensure you have enough space to lay out the large leather piece comfortably. Clear any obstacles or clutter that might hinder your movement during cutting.

- ✓ ***Use a Large Cutting Mat***: Invest in a large cutting mat that provides a smooth and protective surface for your work. The mat helps prevent damage to your cutting tools and provides a stable area for cutting the large piece.
- ✓ ***Secure the Leather***: Use weights, clips, or heavy objects to secure the edges of the leather piece firmly onto the cutting mat. Doing this prevents the leather from shifting or moving during cutting, ensuring more precise cuts.
- ✓ ***Use a Long Straight Edge or Ruler***: When making long straight cuts, use a long straight edge or ruler as a guide to maintain a straight cutting line. This helps you achieve even and accurate cuts across the entire length of the leather.
- ✓ ***Take Your Time***: Cutting large pieces of leather requires patience and focus. Take your time to ensure each cut is deliberate and accurate. Rushing can lead to mistakes or uneven cuts.
- ✓ ***Use a Support Stand***: If possible, use a support stand or table to raise the large piece of leather to a more comfortable cutting height. This reduces strain on your back and arms while cutting.

- ✓ ***Work in Sections***: If the entire piece is too large to handle comfortably, consider cutting it into manageable sections. Mark the cutting lines for each section and cut them one at a time.
- ✓ ***Ask for Assistance***: Enlist the help of a friend or fellow leatherworker to assist you in holding and supporting the large piece while you make the cuts. An extra set of hands can make the process smoother and more efficient.
- ✓ ***Use a Rotary Cutter:*** A rotary cutter can be easier to handle for large straight cuts. Its rolling motion reduces the effort required to make long cuts compared to a regular knife.
- ✓ ***Use a Cutting Table:*** If you frequently work with large pieces of leather, consider investing in a dedicated cutting table with a cutting surface that accommodates the size of your projects. A cutting table provides better support and ergonomics for cutting large pieces.

By implementing these strategies, you can overcome the challenges of handling large leather pieces during straight cuts and achieve precise and polished results in your leatherworking projects.

6. *Hand Fatigue*

Cutting leather involves repetitive hand movements, likely leading to hand fatigue over extended periods. Fatigue may affect cutting precision and overall work quality.

To overcome hand fatigue during straight cuts, you can follow these tips:

- ✓ ***Use ergonomic tools:*** Invest in high-quality, ergonomic cutting tools like a rotary cutter with an ergonomic handle that fits comfortably in your hand and reduces strain during prolonged use.
- ✓ ***Take regular breaks***: Schedule short breaks during your leatherworking sessions to rest your hands and prevent excessive strain.
- ✓ ***Stretch and exercise***: Perform hand and wrist stretches before, during, and after your leatherworking sessions to improve flexibility and reduce fatigue.
- ✓ ***Maintain good posture***: Pay attention to your posture while working to minimize stress on your hands and wrists. Sit with proper back support and keep your hands in a neutral position.

- ✓ ***Use a cutting mat***: Work on a soft, self-healing mat to absorb some pressure when cutting, reducing the impact on your hands.
- ✓ ***Grip lightly***: Avoid gripping your cutting tools too tightly; use a relaxed grip to prevent unnecessary strain.
- ✓ ***Alternate hands:*** If possible, switch hands during tasks that involve repetitive movements to give each hand a break.
- ✓ ***Warm-up exercises***: Warm up your hands by gently massaging them or using a warm compress before starting your leatherworking session.
- ✓ ***Consider hand protection***: Wear finger guards or gloves to protect your fingers and reduce friction while working with leather.
- ✓ ***Strengthen hand muscles***: Incorporate hand exercises, like squeezing a stress ball or using hand exercisers, to strengthen the muscles and reduce fatigue over time.

By implementing these measures, you can minimize hand fatigue and enjoy more comfortable and productive leatherworking sessions. Remember that taking care of your hands is essential for the long-term enjoyment of your craft.

7. *Leather Distortion*

Stretching or pulling the leather while straight cutting can distort its shape, leading to inaccurate cuts and difficulty assembling the pieces later in the project.

To overcome the challenge of distorting the leather during straight cuts in leatherworking, you can follow these tips:

- ✓ ***Stabilize the Leather***: Ensure the leather is stable and securely positioned on your work surface before cutting. Use clips or weights to hold the leather in place and prevent it from shifting during cutting.

- ✓ ***Use a Cutting Mat***: Place a cutting mat or self-healing mat under the leather to provide a stable, non-slip surface. The mat will protect both your work surface and the leather from damage.

- ✓ ***Start with Light Pressure***: When making the initial cut, use light pressure on the cutting tool. Doing this allows you to create a guide line without cutting too deeply into the leather, reducing the risk of distortion.

- ✓ ***Cut in Sections***: For longer cuts or complex shapes, consider cutting in sections instead of cutting the entire length simultaneously. This approach allows for more control and precision.

- ✓ ***Use the Right Cutting Tool***: When working with leather, choosing a cutting tool that matches the thickness and type of leather you use is crucial. For thicker leather, a sharp hobby knife or rotary cutter designed for leather will provide cleaner cuts with minimal distortion. Use a sturdy ruler as a guide to ensure straight cuts. However, cutting thin leather can be more challenging, as they are prone to pulling and distortion when using scissors. For you to cut thin leather straight and neatly, it's best to avoid using scissors and opt for a sharp hobby knife instead, along with a steady hand and a ruler to guide your cuts. You'll achieve precise and professional results in your leather projects by selecting the appropriate cutting tool and practicing proper cutting techniques.
- ✓ ***Avoid Serrated Blades***: Serrated blades can snag and pull at the leather, leading to distortion. Opt for a smooth and sharp blade that glides smoothly through the leather.
- ✓ ***Keep the Cutting Line Visible***: Ensure you see the marked cutting line throughout the process. Doing this helps you stay on track and make accurate cuts without veering off course.
- ✓ ***Practice Cutting style***: Improve your cutting style through practice. Develop a steady hand and controlled

cutting motion to minimize the chances of distorting the leather.

✓ ***Cut on Scrap Leather***: If you are uncertain about a particular cut or technique, practice on scrap pieces of leather before working on your main project. This approach allows you to refine your skills and gain confidence.

✓ ***Use a Ruler or Straight Edge***: Use a ruler or straight edge as a guide for long, straight cuts. Doing this helps maintain straight lines and reduces the risk of cutting off the intended path.

By applying these techniques, you can overcome the challenge of distorting the leather during straight cuts and achieve cleaner and more accurate results in your leatherworking projects.

*8. **Difficulty Cutting Thick Leather***

Straight cutting through thick and stiff leather requires more effort and control. This challenge can lead to uneven cuts and potential damage to the leather without proper technique. Straight-cutting thick leather can be challenging, but with the right approach and tools, you can overcome this difficulty.

Here are some strategies to help you straight-cut thick leather more effectively:

- ✓ ***Choose the Right Cutting Tool***: Opt for a sturdy and sharp tool suitable for cutting through thick leather. Heavy-duty leather shears, rotary cutters with sharp blades, or a leather cutting knife with a strong handle can be good options.
- ✓ ***Moisten the Leather:*** Sprinkle a small amount of water on the surface of the leather to slightly dampen it. Doing this can make the leather more pliable and easier to cut through.
- ✓ ***Use a Mallet or Hammer***: For thicker leather, use a mallet or hammer to tap the cutting tool gently, especially for straight cuts. The additional force helps the cutting tool penetrate the leather more effectively.
- ✓ ***Cut in Stages***: Instead of attempting to cut through thick leather in one go, make multiple passes to deepen the cut gradually. This technique prevents the cutting tool from getting stuck and allows for cleaner cuts.
- ✓ ***Be Patient and Steady:*** Cutting through thick leather requires patience and a steady hand. Apply even pressure and use slow, deliberate motions to ensure clean and accurate cuts.

- ✓ ***Support the Leather:*** Place a cutting mat or a piece of scrap wood under the leather to provide support and prevent the blade from hitting a hard surface, which could damage the blade or cause uneven cuts.
- ✓ ***Consider a Leather Splitter***: A leather splitter is a specialized tool that gradually removes thick leather by reducing its thickness. Investing in a leather splitter can significantly ease cutting if you frequently work with thick leather.
- ✓ ***Use a Ruler or Straight Edge***: When making straight cuts, use a ruler or straight edge as a guide to maintain a straight and consistent cutting line.
- ✓ ***Take Breaks***: Cutting thick leather is physically demanding. Take short breaks to rest your hand and avoid fatigue, as tired hands can lead to less precise cuts.
- ✓ ***Sharpen Cutting*** Tools: Regularly check and sharpen your cutting tools to ensure they perform best. Dull tools can make cutting thick leather even more difficult.

Remember, cutting thick leather may require more effort and practice. Still, with time and experience, you'll develop the skills to handle this challenge effectively and achieve high-quality results in your leatherworking projects.

Practice is essential to overcome these challenges. Gradually improve your cutting skills through repeated practice on scrap leather before working on your main projects. Additionally, investing in high-quality cutting tools, maintaining sharp blades, and using cutting guides or rulers can greatly improve the accuracy and precision of your straight cuts. With patience and persistence, you'll develop the proficiency to create clean and professional-looking straight cuts in leatherworking.

Let's explore how to make straight Cuts:

- **Steps for Making Straight Cuts**

✓ ***Step 1:***

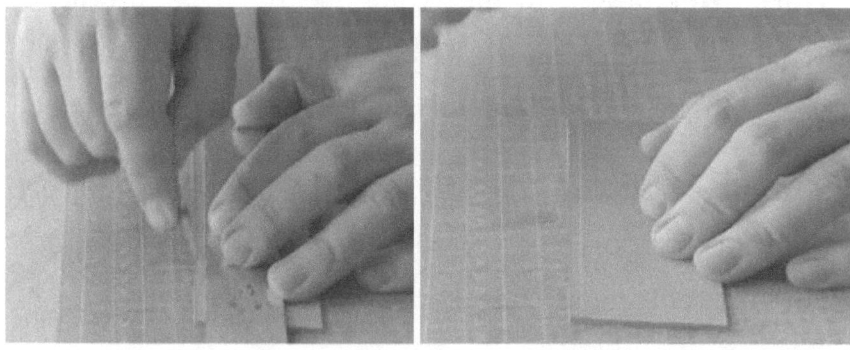

Measure and mark the desired length or shape on the leather using a ruler and a leather marking pen or awl. To do it better, use a sharp marking tool and make clear, precise markings. Take your time to double-check the measurements and alignment to avoid errors.

✓ ***Step 2:***

Hold the cutting tool firmly in your dominant hand, such as a sharp leather cutting knife or rotary cutter. Maintaining a proper grip on the cutting tool for improved control and safety. Ensure the blade is sharp to achieve cleaner cuts with less effort.

✓ ***Step 3:***

Align the cutting tool with the marked line, ensuring it stays perpendicular to the leather surface. Take extra care to align the tool accurately along the markings to avoid deviations during cutting.

✓ ***Step 4:***

As you apply even pressure, make a smooth, continuous cut along the marked line. Focus on maintaining a steady cutting motion without applying excessive force. A smooth cut will prevent jagged edges and uneven results.

✓ ***Step 5:***

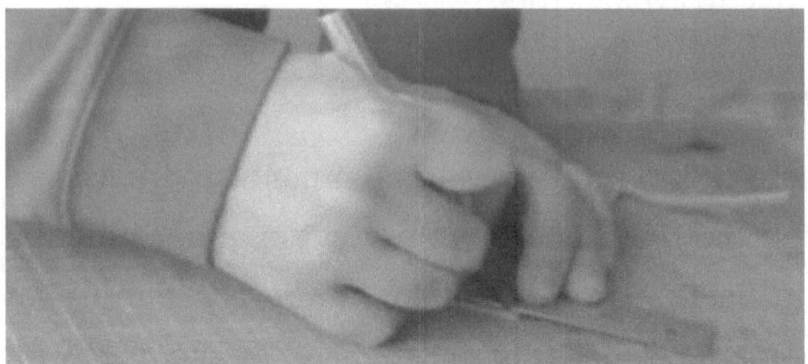

For longer cuts, consider using a straight edge or ruler as a guide to maintain straightness. This technique will help you achieve longer, and straighter cuts with better precision. Use a ruler or straight edge that securely stays in place while cutting.

✓ ***Step 6:***

Practice cutting on scrap leather to improve your cutting skills and gain confidence before working on your main project. Regular practice will enhance your cutting techniques and increase your comfort with the tools. Use different scrap pieces to practice straight and curved cuts to master various cutting styles.

Mastering straight-cutting techniques is essential for any aspiring leatherworker. It allows you to efficiently create precise and clean cuts, paving the way for crafting a wide range of leather projects, from belts and wallets to bags and accessories. By honing your straight-cut skills, you set the foundation for further exploring more intricate cutting techniques and advancing your leatherworking journey.

Now, let's move on to explore curved cuts:

Curved Cuts

Curved cuts create smooth and precise cuts along curved lines or shapes on a piece of leather.

Unlike straight cuts, which are linear and straightforward, curved cuts require more finesse and control to achieve the desired shape. This method is essential for crafting leather projects that involve intricate designs, decorative elements, or items with rounded edges.

- **How Curved Cuts Can Be Applied in Leatherworking**

Curved cuts can be used in various leatherworking projects to add visual appeal, complexity, and uniqueness to the final piece.

Here are some examples of how curved cuts can be used:

- ✓ ***Decorative Patterns*:** Curved cuts are often employed to create intricate and eye-catching patterns on leather surfaces. These patterns can range from simple floral designs to more elaborate motifs, enhancing the overall aesthetics of the leather item.

- ✓ ***Shaping and Contouring*:** When crafting items like leather armor, bags, or saddles, curved cuts shape and contour the leather to fit the intended form. These cuts allow leather pieces to mold and conform to the wearer's curves or the covered object.

- ✓ ***Leather Accessories*:** Curved cuts create small leather accessories such as keychains, bracelets, and earrings. These cuts add intricacy and elegance to these smaller pieces.

- ✓ ***Edges and Trims*:** Curved cuts are commonly used to shape leather projects' edges and trims. Wallets, belts, and sheaths are examples of items that may require curved cuts to achieve smooth and rounded edges.

- **Overcoming Challenges in Making Curved Cuts In Leather**

When making curved cuts in leather, you may encounter several challenges.

Here are some of these challenges, along with their corresponding solutions:

✓ ***Dealing with Complex Designs***

It is challenging to make precise curved cuts when working on projects with intricate and complex designs.

To overcome this challenge:

1) Break down the design into smaller sections and cut one segment at a time.

2) Use the template or marking lines to guide each cut carefully.

3) Additionally, practice on scrap leather to better understand how to approach and execute the more complex curves.

✓ *Maintaining Consistency*

Achieving consistency in curved cuts is crucial for a professional and polished look. Inconsistent cuts can disrupt the overall aesthetics of the leather item.

To address this challenge:

1) Focus on maintaining a steady cutting pace and pressure throughout the cutting process.

2) Take breaks to avoid fatigue, which can lead to uneven cuts.

✓ *Handling Different Types of Leather*

Different types of leather have varying thicknesses and textures, which can pose challenges during curved cutting.

Overcome this hurdle by adjusting the cutting tool and technique based on the specific leather type. You may need to apply more pressure and make slower cuts for thicker leather, while thinner leather might require a lighter touch.

✓ *Addressing Curves in Tight Spaces*

Curves in tight or confined spaces are particularly challenging to cut accurately.

To overcome this:

1) Consider using smaller cutting tools or blades that provide better maneuverability.

2) You can also experiment with different cutting angles to achieve precise cuts in tight corners.

By addressing these unique challenges in curved cuts, you can improve your skills and create beautiful, intricate leather projects that showcase your craftsmanship and creativity. Always take your time, practice, and seek inspiration from other experienced leatherworkers.

And how do you achieve curved cuts?

- **Step for Making Curved Cuts**

✓ ***Step 1:***

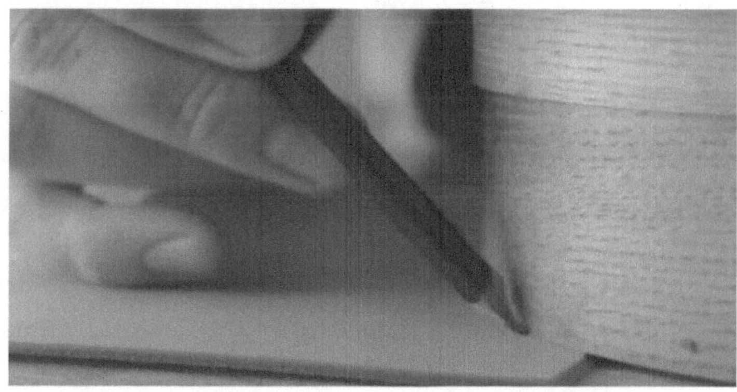

Mark the desired curve or shape on the leather using a template or lightly drawn lines with a pencil. Take your time to get the curve just right. To improve your curve marking, use a flexible curve ruler or specialized templates to achieve precise and consistent curves. Ensure the markings are clear and easily visible, especially for intricate designs.

✓ ***Step 2:***

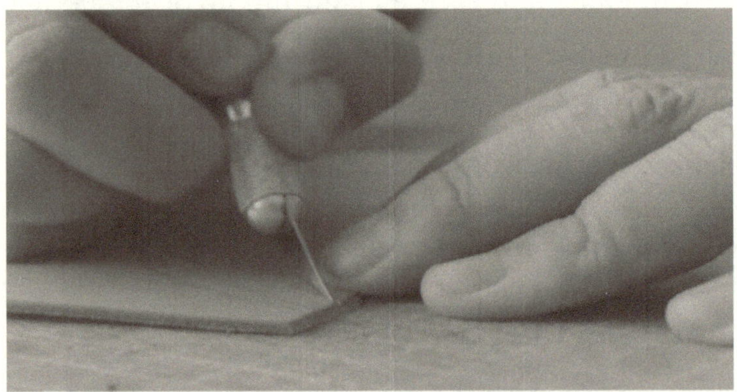

Hold the cutting tool at a slight angle, allowing the blade to follow the curve smoothly. Use your non-dominant hand to guide and stabilize the leather. To enhance stability, practice maintaining a steady hand and a proper grip on the cutting tool. Keep the blade's angle consistent as you cut along the curve.

✓ ***Step 3:***

Make small, controlled cuts along the marked curve, adjusting the angle of the tool as necessary to maintain accuracy and prevent slipping. Ensure the blade is sharp and use gentle, controlled movements to avoid cutting too deep or deviating from the marked curve.

✓ ***Step 4:***

Take your time and cut slowly, ensuring each cut is clean and follows the desired curve. Rushing may lead to mistakes or uneven cuts. Be patient and maintain focus on achieving smooth and accurate cuts. Stop periodically to reposition your hand and retain control over the cutting tool if needed.

✓ ***Step 5:***

Practice on scrap leather with different curve shapes to improve your proficiency. Experiment with various cutting techniques and tools on scrap pieces to build confidence and refine your skills. Gradually progress to more complex curves as your proficiency improves. Regular practice will help you achieve consistent and precise curved cuts in your leatherworking projects.

Mastering leather-cutting techniques is crucial for every leatherworker. Straight cuts ensure efficiency, reducing waste and creating clean edges for projects. Curved cuts add complexity and visual appeal, making leather pieces stand out. Whether crafting belts, wallets, bags, or accessories, practicing these techniques will lead to exquisite results. Attention to detail and consistent practice will elevate your leatherworking craftsmanship.

Now, let's explore how to perfect the other steps involved in leatherworking.

Chapter 5: Step 2-Stitching

You will need to stitch to join leather pieces together and add strength and aesthetics to the final product.

Let's explore the two common stitching methods, which are:

✓ Hand stitching

✓ Machine stitching

Hand Stitching

Hand stitching in leatherworking is a fundamental technique used in various stages of crafting leather goods. It involves using needles and thread to combine leather pieces, create decorative elements, and add functional details to the final product.

- **Application of Hand Stitching**

Hand stitching is commonly used in the following scenarios:

✓ ***Assembling Leather Pieces*:** Hand stitching is used to join different parts of a leather project together, such as stitching together panels to form a bag, wallet, or other accessories. This technique provides a secure and durable bond.

- ✓ ***Creating Leather Seams*:** Hand stitching is crucial for creating seams on leather items. Depending on the project, different stitches, such as saddle or running stitches, help achieve strong and neat seams.

- ✓ ***Adding Decorative Accents*:** Leather artisans often use hand stitching to add decorative elements to their leatherwork. These elements could include stitching patterns, embossed designs, or contrasting thread colors for aesthetic appeal.

- ✓ ***Attaching Hardware***: Hand stitching is employed to attach hardware components like buckles, clasps, or buttons to leather items. This ensures that the hardware is securely in place.

- ✓ ***Repairing Leather Goods*:** Hand stitching is also helpful in repairing leather items that may have worn out or suffered damage over time. Skilled artisans can mend tears or replace worn-out stitches to extend the product's life.

- ✓ ***Leather Tooling*:** Hand stitching can be combined with leather tooling techniques, such as carving or stamping, to create intricate and unique designs on the leather surface.

✓ ***Finishing Touches*:** Hand stitching is often the final step in completing a leather project. It gives your creations a polished and refined appearance, demonstrating the craftsmanship and attention to detail that sets your work apart. Hand stitching plays a crucial role in joining leather pieces securely and creating durable seams, whether you're crafting a simple keychain, a stylish wristband, or a functional cardholder.

As a beginner, mastering hand stitching allows you to add a personal touch to your leather goods and create unique and one-of-a-kind pieces. Hand stitching allows for precise and meticulous work, making it suitable for intricate designs and high-quality leather goods. It offers a level of control and attention to detail that many leatherworkers and enthusiasts prefer. It also adds a sense of craftsmanship and authenticity to the finished product. Whether for functional purposes, artistic expressions, or repairing cherished leather items, hand stitching remains a timeless and essential skill in leatherworking.

- **Overcoming Challenges in Hand Stitching**

Hand stitching in leatherworking is rewarding but has its fair share of challenges.

Here are some common challenges you may face when hand stitching leather, along with strategies to overcome them:

✓ ***Needle Breakage***

The needle may break or bend while stitching through thick or tough leather.

To overcome this:

1) Use high-quality needles suitable for leatherworking.
2) Avoid forcing the needle through the material. If you encounter significant resistance, try using a stitching awl to create pilot holes before stitching.

✓ ***Uneven Stitches***

Keeping your stitches even and consistent can be challenging, especially for beginners.

To improve your stitching, practice regularly and use techniques like marking stitch lines with a ruler or a wing divider to create evenly spaced guides for hand-sewing.

✓ ***Knots and Tangles***

Tying knots at the beginning and end of your stitches can lead to tangles and messy finishes.

To avoid this, use a simple loop or saddle stitch technique, and leave enough thread at the start and end to secure without bulky knots.

✓ ***Thread Fraying***

Low-quality or improperly conditioned thread may fray during stitching.

Therefore, choose strong and waxed threads suitable for leatherwork, and keep the thread ends tidy and waxed to minimize fraying.

✓ ***Hand Fatigue***

Hand stitching can be time-consuming, leading to hand fatigue and strain.

To avoid this challenge:

1) Take breaks during extended stitching sessions to rest your hands and prevent overexertion.

2) Consider using thimbles or finger guards to protect your fingers from excessive pressure.

✓ ***Misaligned Stitches***

Keeping your stitches straight and aligned can be tricky, mainly when working with complex patterns or curves.

To avoid this challenge, use clips or tape to hold the pieces together and ensure precise alignment before stitching.

✓ ***Stitching Through Multiple Layers***

When stitching through multiple layers of thick leather, you may encounter difficulty pulling the needle and thread through.

To avoid this, try using pliers to grip the needle and gently pull it through the layers.

✓ ***Backstitching Neatly***

Neatly backstitching at the end of a seam can be challenging, as it requires blending the stitches seamlessly.

Therefore, practice the backstitch technique and experiment with different ways to secure the end of your stitches neatly.

✓ ***Stitching Curves***

Stitching along curves can be tough to maintain, even stitch length and alignment.

To improve your curved stitching, use your non-dominant hand to guide the leather smoothly while maintaining an even pace.

Overcoming these challenges in hand stitching requires practice, patience, and attention to detail. With time and dedication, you'll develop the skills to handle these obstacles and create beautifully hand-stitched leather projects. Remember to start with more straightforward projects and gradually progress to more complex ones as your stitching proficiency grows.

- **How to Make Hand Stitches**

Here is the process for hand stitching:

1. ***Prepare the Leather Pieces***

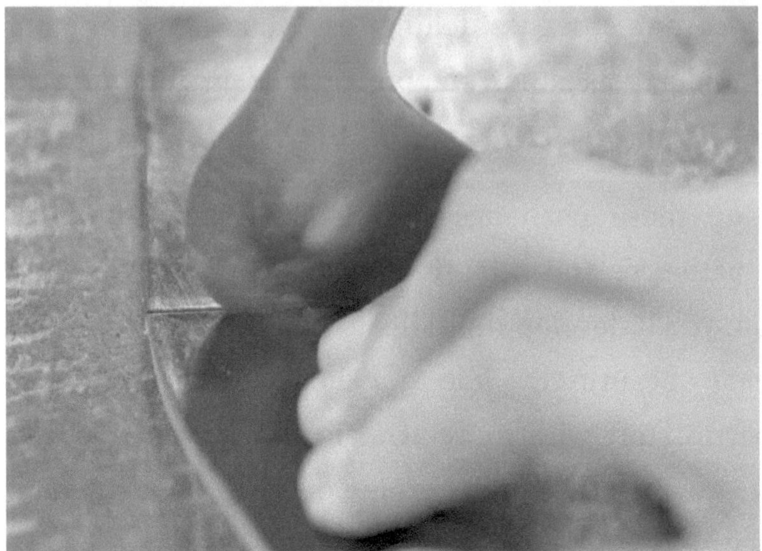

Use the guidelines we learned in the previous chapter to cut your leather.

2. *Mark Stitching Lines*

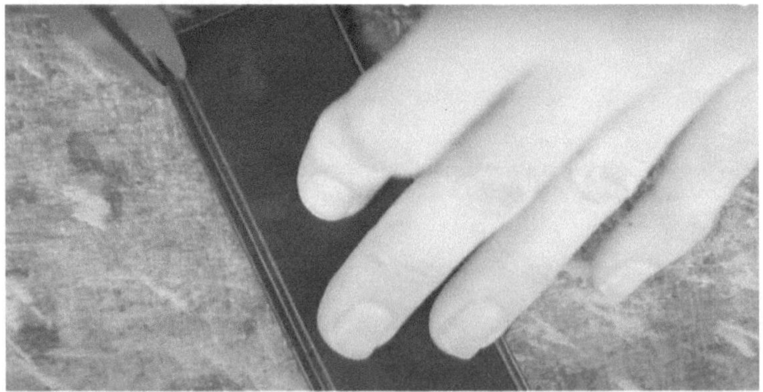

To create even stitching lines, utilize a wing divider or compass to mark the leather precisely. Make these markings lightly with a pencil to guide your stitching without leaving permanent marks on the leather. Ensure the stitching lines are straight and properly aligned with the edges of the leather to achieve a professional finish.

3. *Create Stitching Holes*

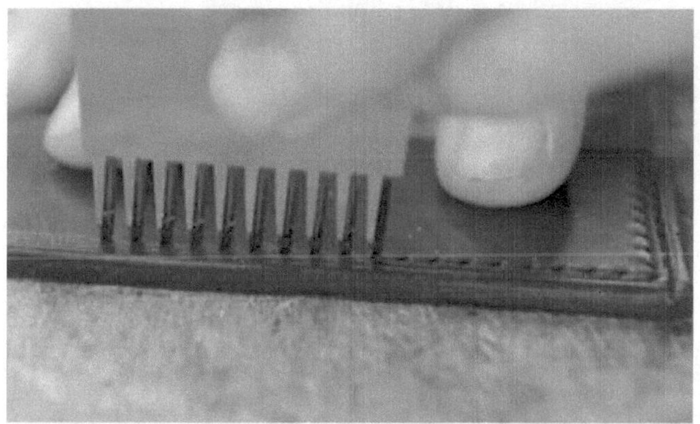

When making stitching holes, choose an appropriate awl or stitching chisel size based on the thread you are using. Apply consistent, steady pressure to create clean, evenly spaced holes along the marked lines. Before proceeding, double-check the spacing between the holes to ensure they are all equidistant, which is essential for achieving a neat stitch.

4. Thread the Needle

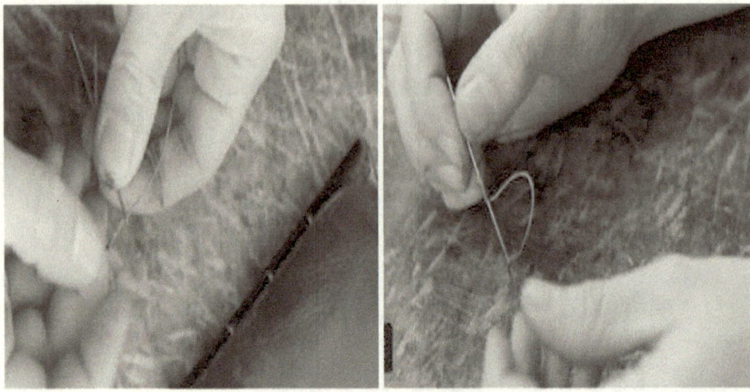

Select a needle with an eye suitable for the thickness of your chosen thread. Threading the needle can be made easier by waxing the thread, which prevents tangling and increases the thread's durability. Thread the needle with a thread length approximately three times the length of your stitching line. Leave enough thread tail at the starting point, ensuring adequate length for later securing the thread.

5. Start Stitching

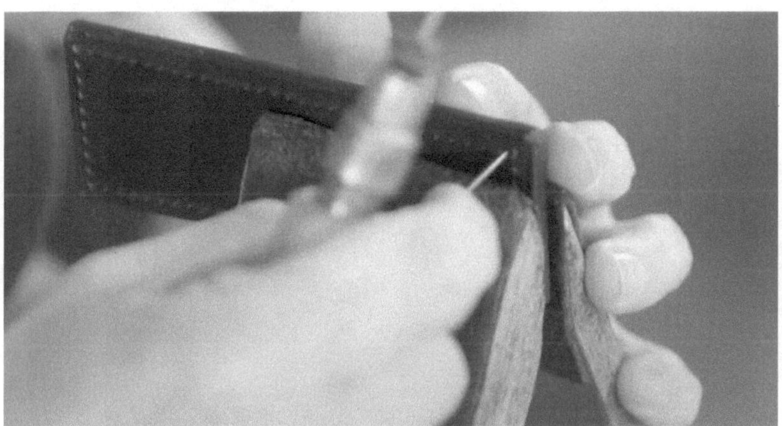

When starting the stitching, insert the needle from the inside of the leather to the outside through the first stitching hole. Leave a short thread tail inside, which you will secure later. Make sure to align the leather pieces accurately and hold them firmly to avoid misalignment during stitching.

6. Stitching Pattern

Choose a stitching pattern that suits your project. The most common stitches for hand stitching are the saddle stitch and the running stitch.

✓ Saddle Stitch

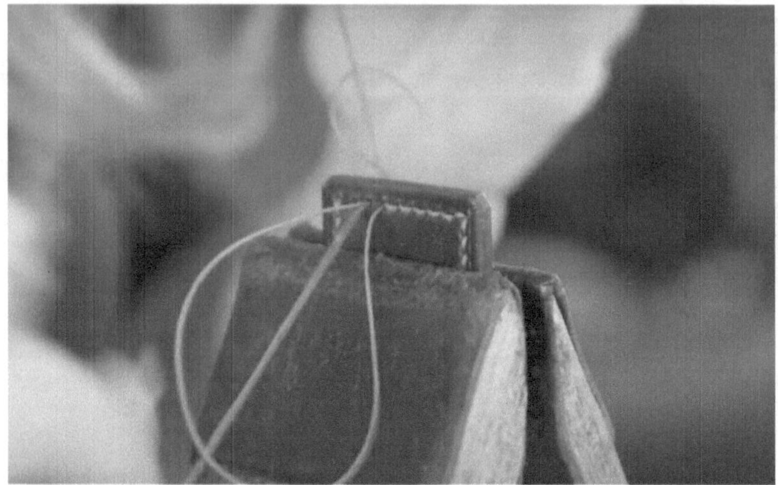

Pass the needle through the next hole from the outside (the grain side) and pull it tight. Then, insert the needle through the previous hole from the inside and pull it tight again. Repeat this process until you reach the end of the stitching line.

✓ Running Stitch

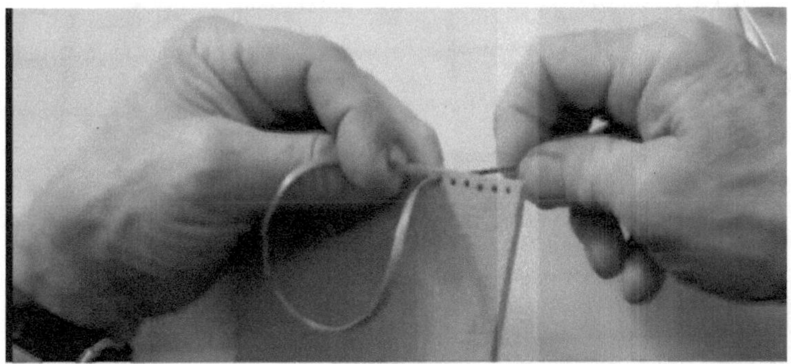

Pass the needle in and out of each hole along the stitching line, creating a continuous line of stitches. This is a simple and quick stitch suitable for lightweight projects.

7. *Tying Off the Thread*

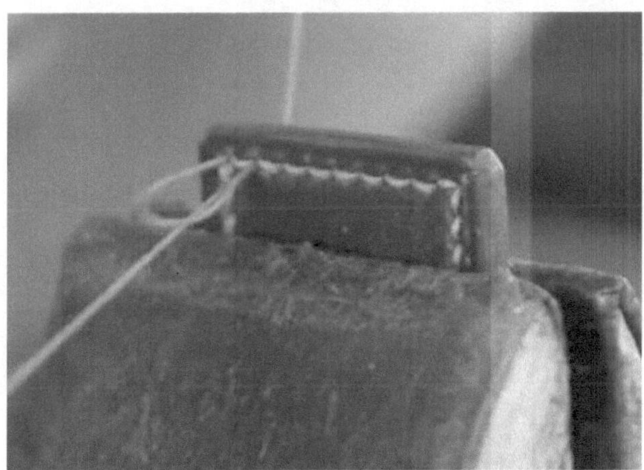

When you reach the end of the stitching line, insert the needle through the last hole and pull it tight. Create a loop with the thread and pass the needle through it to form a knot.

Tighten the knot by pulling the thread gently. This will secure the stitching and prevent it from unraveling.

8. Securing the Knot

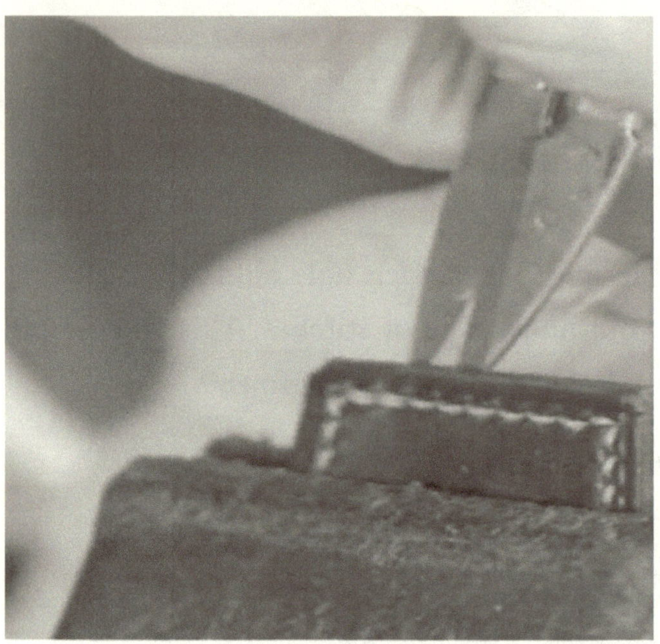

To secure the knot, pass the needle between the two leather layers and trim the excess thread close to the leather surface. The trimmed end will be hidden between the layers, creating a neat finish. Make sure the knot is tight and secure to prevent it from unraveling.

9. Finishing

Inspect your stitching for any loose stitches or areas that need reinforcement. Trim any excess thread and ensure the stitches are tight and even. If your project has multiple stitching lines or additional pieces to attach, repeat the process as needed.

With practice, your hand-stitching skills in leatherworking will improve, and you'll be able to create more intricate and professional-looking leather projects. Enjoy the process and have fun with your leatherworking journey!

Machine Stitching

Machine stitching, also known as ***sewing***, is a method of joining leather pieces using a sewing machine. In leatherworking, a sewing machine equipped with a leather-specific needle and thread is used to create strong and precise stitches in leather projects. This technique is commonly used when efficiency and speed are required, especially in large-scale production or projects involving long seams.

- **Application of Machine Stitching**

Machine stitching is suitable for a wide range of leather items, including:

✓ ***Leather Garments***: Sewing is commonly used to create leather jackets, vests, pants, and other clothing items.

- ✓ ***Leather Bags and Accessories***: Handbags, backpacks, wallets, and other leather accessories often feature machine-stitched seams.
- ✓ ***Upholstery***: In furniture upholstery, sewing machines stitch leather covers for sofas, chairs, and other seating pieces.
- ✓ ***Leather Goods***: Many leather goods, such as belts, watch straps, and keychains, are produced using machine stitching.
- ✓ ***Automotive Upholstery***: In the automotive industry, leather interiors and seat covers are often machine-stitched.
- ✓ ***Footwear***: Some leather footwear, like leather boots and shoes, are machine-stitched for efficiency.

Machine stitching is highly efficient and can produce consistent results, making it ideal for mass production and commercial leather goods manufacturing. However, hand-stitching is preferred for certain high-end and bespoke leather items due to its artisanal touch and ability to create unique designs and patterns.

Machine stitching in leatherworking comes with challenges, but with proper techniques and attention to detail, these challenges can be overcome.

- **Overcoming Challenges in Machine Stitching**

Here are some common challenges you might encounter when machine stitching leather, along with tips on how to overcome them:

✓ ***Needle Breakage***

Leather is a dense and tough material, sometimes leading to needle breakage, especially if the sewing machine is not equipped with a heavy-duty needle.

To overcome this:

1. Ensure that you use the correct needle type specifically designed for sewing leather.
2. Additionally, reduce the machine's stitching speed and use proper thread tension to minimize stress on the needle.

✓ ***Thread Tangles***

The thickness and nature of leather thread can cause tangling or knotting while stitching.

To avoid this:

1. Use high-quality, waxed, or nylon thread suitable for leatherwork.

2. Also, ensure the thread tension is adjusted correctly to prevent snags and tangles during stitching.

✓ ***Uneven Stitching***

Inconsistent stitch length or tension can result in uneven stitching, affecting the overall appearance and durability of the leather item.

To avoid this, regularly check and adjust the thread tension and stitch length according to the leather thickness and the sewing machine's capabilities.

✓ ***Skipped Stitches***

Sometimes, the sewing machine may skip stitches due to the density of the leather.

To avoid this challenge:

1. Ensure the leather pieces are correctly aligned and securely placed using clips or clamps to prevent skipping.

2. Adjusting the machine's needle position or using a walking foot attachment can also help.

✓ *Leather Movement*

Leather tends to be slippery, leading to uneven feeding and shifting while stitching.

Use an appropriate non-slip sewing machine foot to keep the leather stable and prevent unnecessary movement during stitching.

✓ *Stitching Straight Lines*

Keeping a straight stitching line on leather can be challenging, especially for longer seams.

Use a ruler or sewing guide to ensure straight lines and maintain a steady hand while guiding the leather through the machine.

✓ *Stitching Thick Leather*

Sewing through thick leather can strain the machine's motor and cause inconsistent stitching.

To avoid this, use a heavy-duty sewing machine designed for leatherwork and, if needed, hand-crank the machine through thicker sections to maintain control.

✓ *Finishing the Stitching*

Properly securing the stitching at the beginning and end of a seam is crucial to prevent unraveling. Therefore, backstitch at the beginning and end of each seam or manually tie off and secure the thread to ensure a strong and durable stitch line.

By understanding these challenges and implementing the suggested solutions, you can achieve smooth and professional machine-stitched leather projects while preserving the integrity and appearance of the leather material. Regular sewing machine maintenance, such as cleaning and lubricating, is vital in ensuring smooth and efficient stitching.

Let's explore the process of machine stitching:

- **Machine Stitching Process**

1. ***Prepare the Leather Pieces***

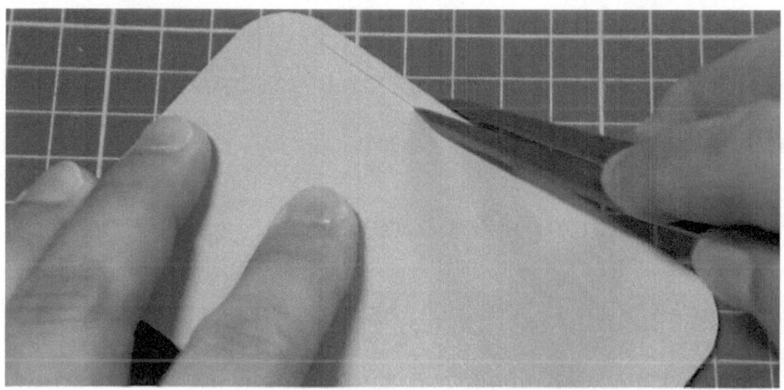

Cut the leather as per the guidelines we have already learned.

2. ***Mark Stitching Lines***

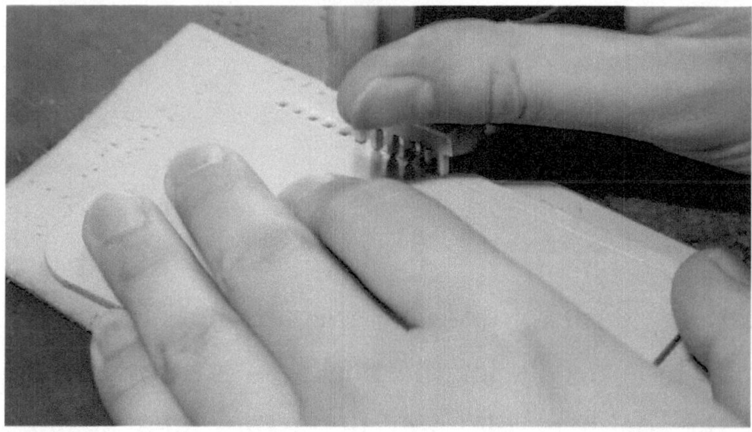

Mark stitching lines on the leather pieces using a wing divider or compass to achieve even stitching. Alternatively, you can use a ruler and a pencil to mark the lines lightly.

Take care to measure and mark the lines accurately, as any discrepancies in the stitching lines can lead to uneven stitches. Using a wing divider or compass helps ensure consistent spacing between the stitches. Use a template or draw the lines freehand with a steady hand for curved stitching lines.

3. *Set Up the Stitching Machine*

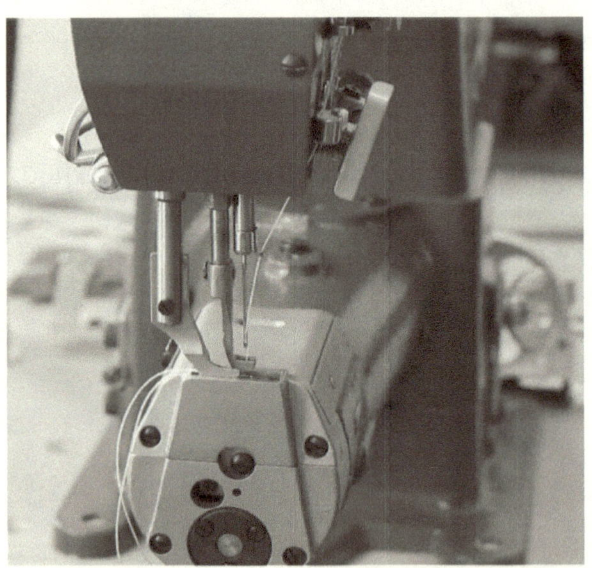

Before starting, ensure you have the appropriate leather stitching machine needle for the thickness of your leather. Choosing the right needle prevents issues like skipped stitches or broken threads. Thread the machine with the selected thread, whether it's waxed thread or nylon thread. Ensure the thread is properly threaded through the machine's tension disks and guides to prevent tangles and thread breakage.

4. Adjust Machine Settings

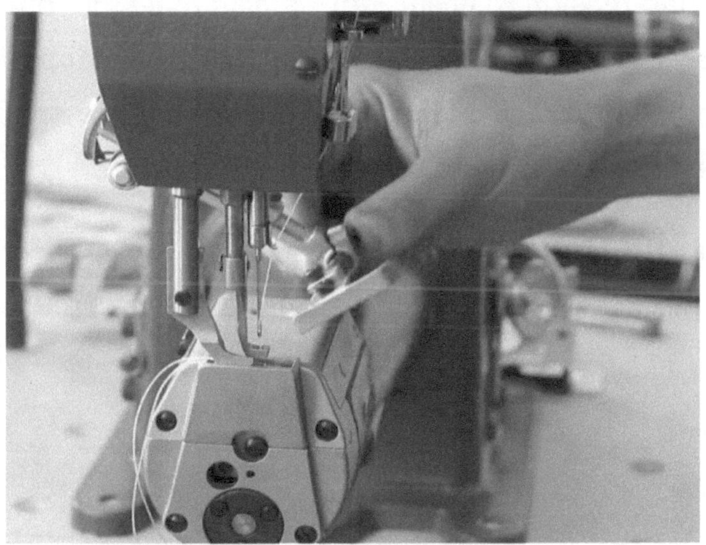

Properly adjust the machine settings to achieve the desired stitch length and tension. For most leather projects, ***a stitch length of 6 to 8 stitches per inch (SPI) is suitable***. Longer stitches may be used for thicker leather, while shorter stitches may be better for lightweight leather. Consult your machine's manual for guidance on adjusting stitch length and tension. Test the settings on a scrap piece of leather and adjust for even and balanced stitches.

5. *Test Stitching*

Perform a test stitch on a scrap piece of leather to ensure the machine is set up correctly and the stitching looks neat. Test stitch length and tension to ensure they are suitable for your project. Inspect the test stitch for loose, tight, or skipped stitches or thread breakage. Make any necessary adjustments before proceeding to your main project.

6. *Position and Hold the Leather*

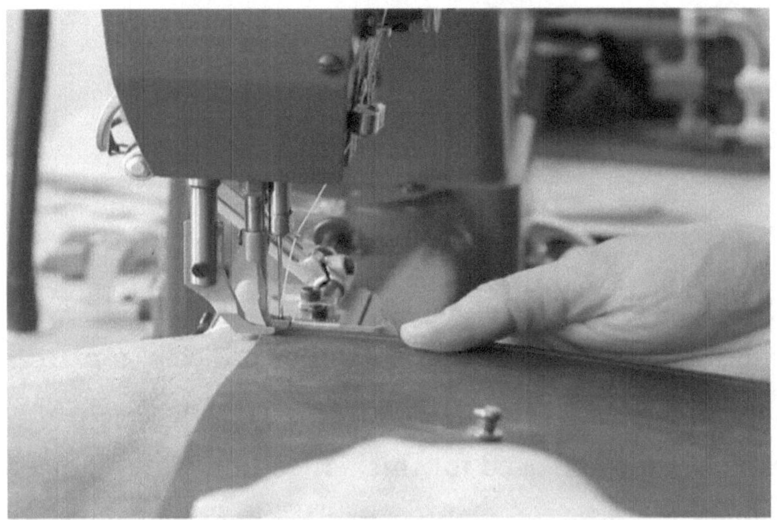

Position the leather pieces to be stitched together, aligning the edges along the marked stitching line. Use clips, clothespins, or double-sided tape to hold the leather pieces securely. This prevents the leather from shifting while you stitch and ensures a straight stitch line. Make sure the edges are evenly aligned for a neat appearance.

7. Start Stitching

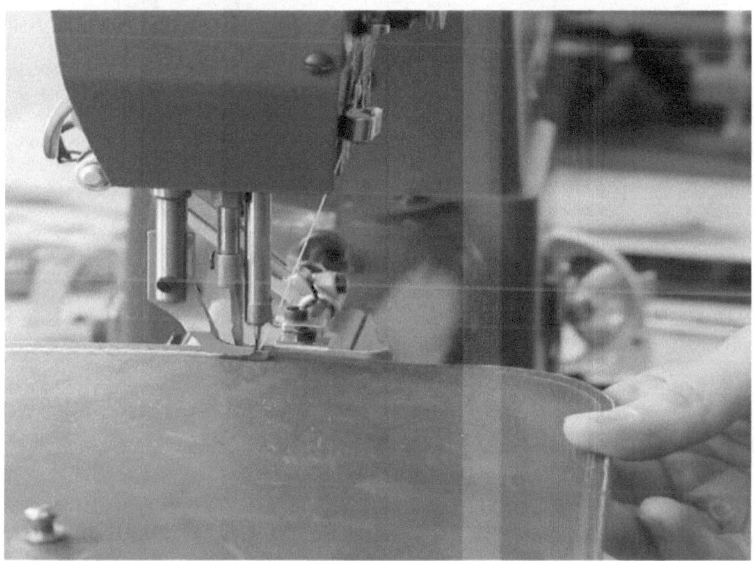

Carefully guide the leather through the sewing machine, following the marked stitching line or keeping a consistent distance from the edge if you didn't mark lines. Use both hands to guide the leather through the machine, keeping it straight and aligned with the needle. Avoid forcefully pulling or pushing the leather, leading to uneven stitching.

8. Machine Stitching Techniques

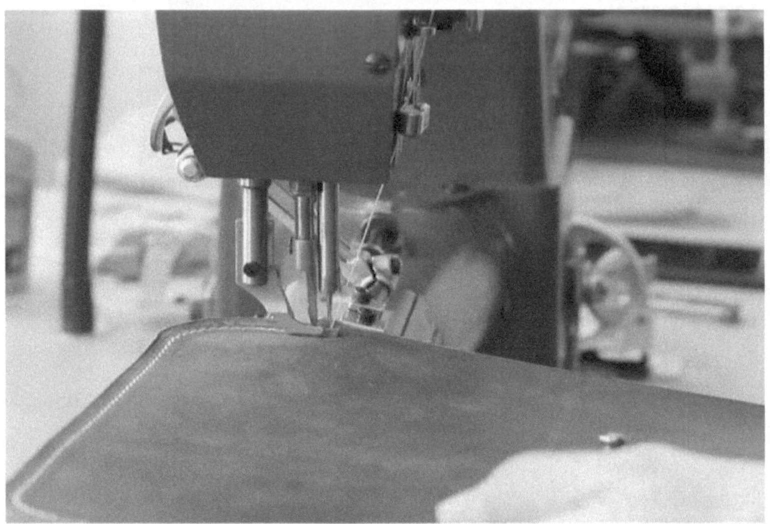

As you stitch, maintain a steady and even pace to allow the machine to feed the leather smoothly. Use proper hand placement to guide the leather through the machine, ensuring a straight and consistent stitch line. Keep your eyes on the stitching line ahead of the needle to help you stay on track. A walking foot attachment will help feed the leather layers evenly and prevent shifting.

9. Finishing

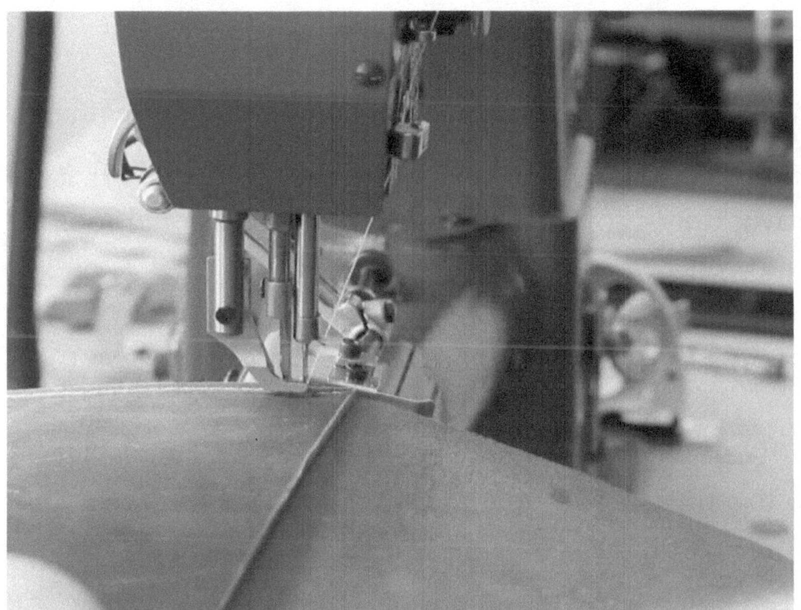

When you reach the end of the stitching line, backstitch a few stitches to secure the thread. Trim any excess thread neatly using sharp scissors or thread snips. Ensure the stitches are evenly spaced and free from tangles or loops. If the stitching line ends in a tight corner, take extra care to backstitch and secure the thread properly.

10. Practice and Patience

Machine stitching in leatherworking takes practice, so be patient with yourself as you develop your skills. Regular practice will improve your stitching precision and speed. As you gain experience, you'll become more confident handling different leather thicknesses and navigating curves and corners.

By paying attention to these details and practicing regularly, you can achieve well-executed machine stitching in your leatherworking projects, resulting in professional-looking and durable leather goods.

Leather Stitching Techniques

There are several stitching techniques used to join leather pieces together. Each method offers different looks and strengths.

Here are some common stitching techniques:

- **Saddle Stitch**

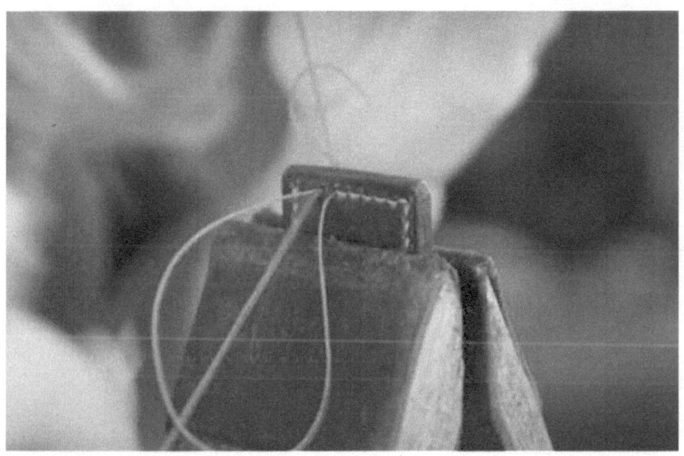

As discussed earlier, saddle stitch is widely ***used in leatherworking to join two leather pieces along their edges***. It provides excellent strength and durability, making it suitable for creating long-lasting and functional leather goods like wallets, belts, sheaths, and small accessories.

To saddle stitch:

1. ***Thread your needles***: Cut a length of waxed thread and thread it through two needles. Ensure the thread is long enough to sew the entire seam without running out.
2. ***Align the leather pieces***: Place the two pieces of leather to be stitched together, aligning the edges evenly.

3. ***Insert the needles***: Insert one needle through the first stitch hole from the inside of the leather and the other through the same hole from the outside. The needles should cross each other inside the leather.

4. ***Cross the needles***: Pull the needles gently to cross them inside the leather.

5. ***Stitch the seam***: Insert each needle through the next stitch hole on the opposite side. Pull the thread tight to secure the stitches.

6. ***Repeat the process***: Continue stitching in this manner until you reach the end of the seam.

7. ***Tie off the thread:*** To secure the stitches, tie a knot at the end of the seam using both needles.

Saddle stitch is suitable for a wide range of leather projects, from small items like keychains and cardholders to larger pieces like belts and wallets.

- **Running Stitch**

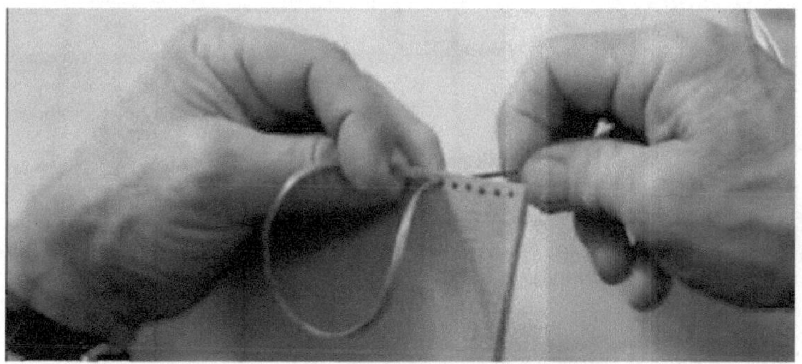

As discussed earlier, a running stitch is a basic and quick hand-sewing technique ***used for temporary or decorative stitching***. While not as strong as other stitching methods, it can hold leather pieces together for testing fit or creating temporary closures.

To execute a running stitch:

1. ***Insert the needle***: Insert the needle through the leather from one side, then pull it up from the opposite side.
2. ***Repeat the process***: Repeat this process to create evenly spaced stitches along the seam.
3. ***Knot the thread:*** Tie a knot at the end of the seam to secure the stitches.

The running stitch is typically used for temporary stitching or to add decorative elements to leather projects where strength is not a primary concern.

- **Backstitch**

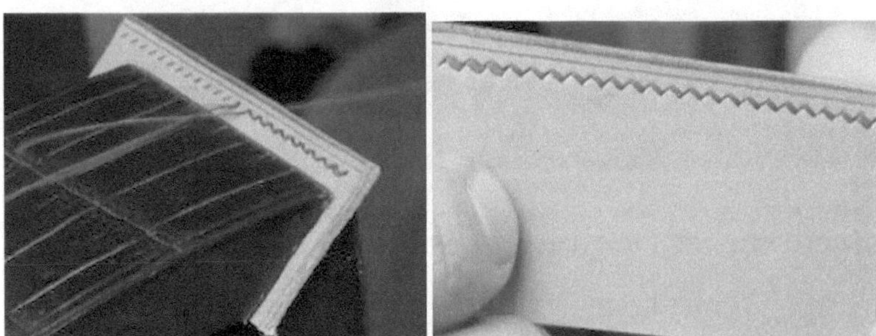

The backstitch is a strong and reliable hand-sewing technique used when durability is essential. ***It is suitable for projects that require extra reinforcement***, like leather bags, heavy-duty straps, and high-wear items.

To backstitch:

1. ***Insert the needle:*** Insert the needle through the leather from one side, then bring it back through the same hole.
2. ***Insert the needle again***: Insert it through the next stitch hole from the front and then pass it back through the previous hole.

3. ***Repeat the process:*** Continue stitching, passing the needle back through the last stitch hole to create a double stitch.

4. ***Knot the thread:*** Tie a knot at the end of the seam to secure the stitches.

Backstitching is commonly used in projects where strength and durability are crucial, such as leather bags, belts, and heavy-duty accessories.

- **Whip Stitch**

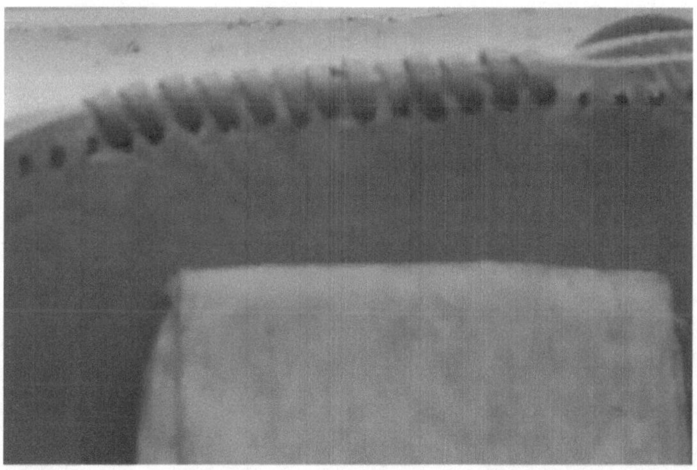

Whipstitch is often ***used for joining leather edges or seams***, especially when working with thinner or softer leather. It creates a decorative and finished appearance along the edges.

To whip stitch:

1. ***Align the edges:*** Align the edges of the leather pieces to be joined.

2. ***Insert the needle:*** Insert it through both layers from one side, and then bring it over the edge and back through both layers from the opposite side.

3. ***Repeat the process:*** Continue stitching along the entire edge to create a series of looping stitches.

4. ***Knot the thread***: Tie a knot at the end of the seam to secure the stitches.

Whip stitching is commonly used for finishing edges on leather projects like pouches, small bags, and decorative leather items.

- **Blanket Stitch**

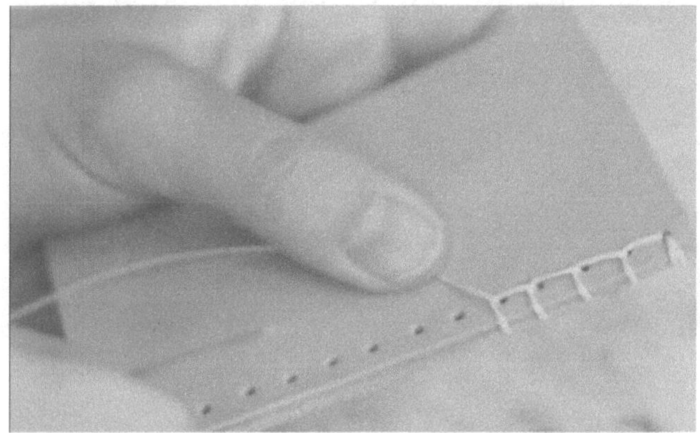

The blanket stitch is ***often used for finishing raw edges or adding decorative borders*** to leather projects. It provides a neat and attractive appearance.

To execute a blanket stitch:

1. ***Insert the needle***: Insert the needle through the leather from one side, leaving a small loop.

2. ***Create the first stitch***: Pass the needle through the loop and pull it tight to create the first stitch.

3. ***Repeat the process:*** Continue along the edge of the leather to create a continuous looped stitch.

4. ***Knot the thread:*** Tie a knot at the end of the seam to secure the stitches.

Blanket stitching is commonly used for finishing raw edges on leather projects like bags, journal covers, and other small accessories.

- **Lock Stitch**

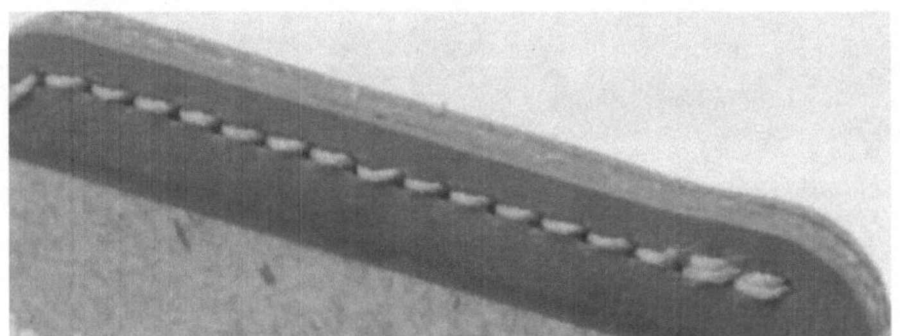

Lock stitch is a machine sewing technique that ***provides a secure and reliable seam in leatherworking***. It is commonly used in manufacturing leather goods.

The lock stitch:

1. ***Set up the machine***: Load the sewing machine with the top thread and bobbin thread.
2. ***Align the leather:*** Align the edges of the leather pieces to be stitched together.
3. ***Sew the seam:*** Stitch along the edge of the leather, ensuring the top and bottom threads interlock to create the lock stitch.

4. ***Knot the thread:*** Tie a knot or backstitch at the end of the seam to secure the stitches.

Lock stitch is commonly used in mass production or when sewing leather pieces where efficiency and consistency are required.

- **Lacing**

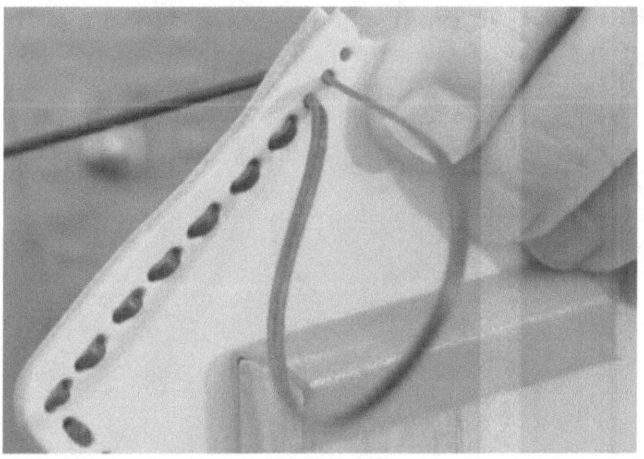

Lacing is a traditional leatherworking technique ***for combining larger leather pieces or creating decorative designs***. It is instrumental when sewing thicker or heavy leather that may be challenging to stitch with needles.

To lace leather:

1. ***Create holes***: Create evenly spaced holes along the edges of the pieces to be joined.

2. ***Lace the leather***: Pass a lace or cord through these holes using an over-and-under pattern, creating a secure and visually appealing finish.

3. ***Knot the ends:*** Tie knots at the ends of the lace to secure the cord or lace.

Lacing is commonly used in projects like leather bags, sheaths, holsters, and decorative leather items where a robust and decorative join is desired.

- **Cross Stitch**

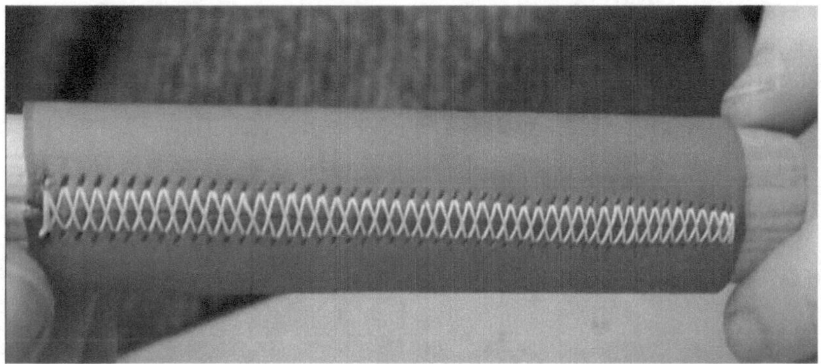

Cross stitch is a decorative hand-sewing technique ***used to create intricate patterns or designs*** on the surface of leather items.

To cross stitch:

1. ***Mark the pattern:*** Mark the pattern or design on the leather surface.
2. ***Insert the needle:*** Insert the needle through the leather from one side, creating one leg of the "X."
3. ***Cross the stitch***: Pass the needle diagonally across the first stitch, then insert it back through the leather to create the second leg of the "X."
4. ***Repeat the process:*** Continue stitching to create a series of "X" shaped stitches on the leather surface.

5. ***Knot the thread:*** Tie a knot at the end of the seam to secure the stitches.

Cross stitching is commonly used for embellishing leather items like book covers, wallets, belts, and decorative leather accessories.

- **Simple Loop**

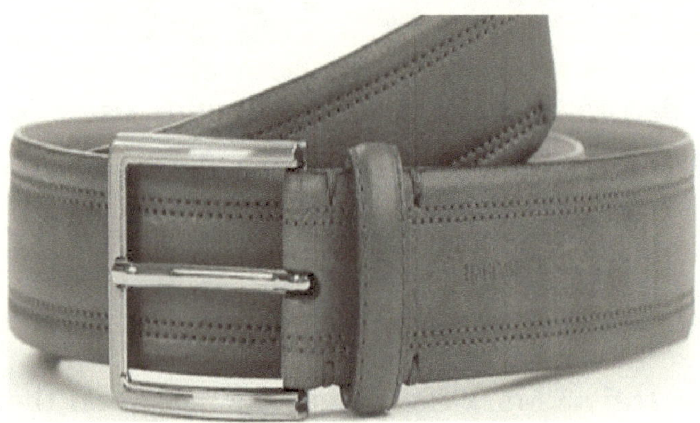

The simple loop is a basic and functional leatherworking technique ***used to create a loop*** for attaching keyrings, clasps, or other fasteners to leather accessories. It is commonly used in projects like keychains, wristbands, and lanyards to provide a secure and convenient way to attach items.

To create a simple loop:

1. ***Cut the leather strip***: Ensure the strip is of the desired length and width, depending on the project's requirements.
2. ***Fold the strip***: Fold the strip in half and secure the two ends together, forming a loop.
3. ***Stitch the loop***: Use a stitching technique like saddle stitch or backstitch to sew the ends together securely.
4. ***Knot the thread***: Tie a knot at the end of the seam to secure the stitches.

Crafting a leather keychain with a simple loop lets you attach keys or small accessories easily, providing a practical and stylish solution for everyday use.

Each stitching technique offers unique characteristics and applications, allowing leatherworkers to choose the most suitable method based on the project's requirements and desired outcome. You can achieve well-crafted leather creations that showcase durability and creativity by mastering these stitching techniques. Practice and experience will help refine your stitching skills and enable you to execute more complex and intricate designs confidently.

Chapter 6: Step 3-Tooling and Leather Stamping

Tooling and leather stamping add intricate designs, texture, and personality to leather creations.

Let's explore this a bit more:

Tooling

Tooling, in the context of leatherworking, refers to creating decorative patterns, designs, or textures on the surface of leather using various hand tools. This technique is commonly used to add visual interest and artistic elements to leather items such as belts, wallets, bags, saddles, and other accessories.

Leather tooling involves using specialized tools, such as stamps, levelers, swivel knives, mallets, and modeling tools, to impress designs into the leather surface. With this, you apply pressure to the tools, creating impressions ranging from simple geometric patterns to intricate floral motifs and complex structures.

Tooling is used for both functional and aesthetic purposes in leatherworking.

- **Common Applications Of Leather Tooling**

✓ ***Embellishment:*** Embellishment refers to adding decorative elements or enhancements to the surface of leather items. Tooling is used to embellish and beautify leather items. Adding embossed patterns and designs enhances the overall aesthetics and gives the leather a more premium and artistic appearance.

✓ ***Personalization:*** Leather artisans can use tooling to customize products with names, initials, or meaningful symbols, making each item unique to the customer.

✓ ***Artistic Expression***: Leather tooling allows artisans to showcase their creativity and craftsmanship, turning plain leather into unique art.

✓ ***Design Highlighting:*** Tooling can emphasize certain areas of a leather item, such as borders, edges, or focal points, drawing attention to specific design elements.

✓ ***Functional Enhancement:*** Besides its decorative purposes, tooling can provide operational benefits, such as creating texture on handles or grips to improve the item's usability and grip.

Tooling is a versatile technique used by leatherworkers to transform plain leather into eye-catching and distinctive pieces, and it remains an essential skill in traditional and contemporary leather crafting.

- **Overcoming Challenges in Leather Tooling**

Tooling leather can be a rewarding but challenging process.

Here are some common challenges that you might face in leather tooling and how to overcome them:

✓ ***Uneven Impressions***: Getting consistent and even impressions while tooling can be tricky, especially for beginners. To overcome this challenge, practice using the leather tool on scrap pieces before working on your main project. Focus on maintaining steady pressure and keeping the tool perpendicular to the leather surface.

✓ ***Over- or Under-Tooling***: It's essential to strike the right balance when tooling leather. Over-tooling can cause the leather to become weak and prone to tearing, while under-tooling may not create the desired effect. Experiment with different pressure levels and practice on scrap leather to find the optimal amount of tooling required.

- ✓ ***Tool Slippage*:** Some leather tools, especially swivel knives, can occasionally slip, leading to unintended marks on the leather. To prevent this, ensure your devices are sharp and in good condition. Also, maintain a secure grip and use tools appropriate for the specific task.

- ✓ ***Design Transfer*:** Transferring complex designs onto the leather can be challenging. To overcome this, use transfer tools, stylus pens, or trace paper to transfer the design accurately onto the leather surface before beginning the tooling process.

- ✓ ***Leather Hardness*:** The hardness of the leather can affect how well it takes impressions. Stiff leather might resist tooling, making it difficult to achieve clear designs. In contrast, soft leather might deform or cut easily under pressure. Choose the right type and thickness of leather for the specific tooling technique you intend to use.

- ✓ ***Patience and Practice*:** Tooling requires patience and practice to master. Don't get discouraged by initial imperfections; keep practicing, and your tooling skills will improve.

- ✓ ***Proper Tool Maintenance*:** Ensure your leather tools are regularly cleaned and sharpened. Dull tools can result in unsatisfactory impressions and make tooling more challenging than it needs to be.

- ✓ ***Choosing the Right Tools*:** Using the appropriate tools for your project is crucial. Invest in high-quality leather tools that match your design requirements, and familiarize yourself with each tool's function and proper usage.

- ✓ ***Personal Safety*:** Leatherworking involves using sharp tools, and accidents can happen. Always prioritize safety by wearing protective gear like gloves and working in a well-ventilated space with proper lighting.

Understanding and addressing these challenges can enhance your tooling skills and create beautifully embellished leather items with precision and finesse. Remember that tooling is an art that requires continuous learning and refinement, so embrace the learning process and enjoy the creative journey.

• Leather Tooling Process

Below is the process:

1. *Prepare the Leather*

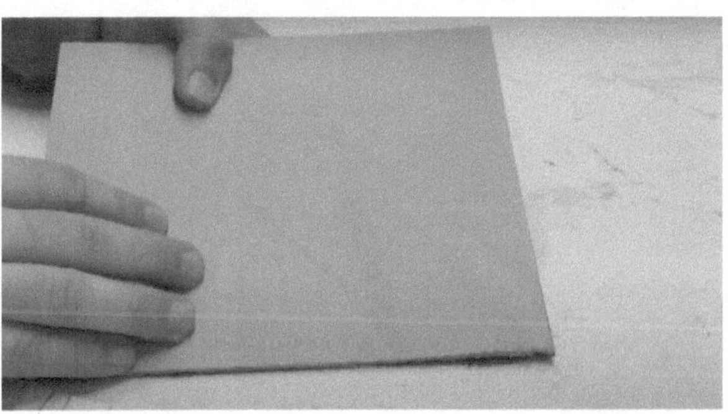

Starting with a piece of leather suitable for tooling is essential for a beginner. Look for smooth and firm leather, such as vegetable-tanned leather, as it will yield better tooling results. Before purchasing a large piece, practice on a smaller scrap of the same type of leather to gain confidence and refine your technique.

2. Dampen the Leather

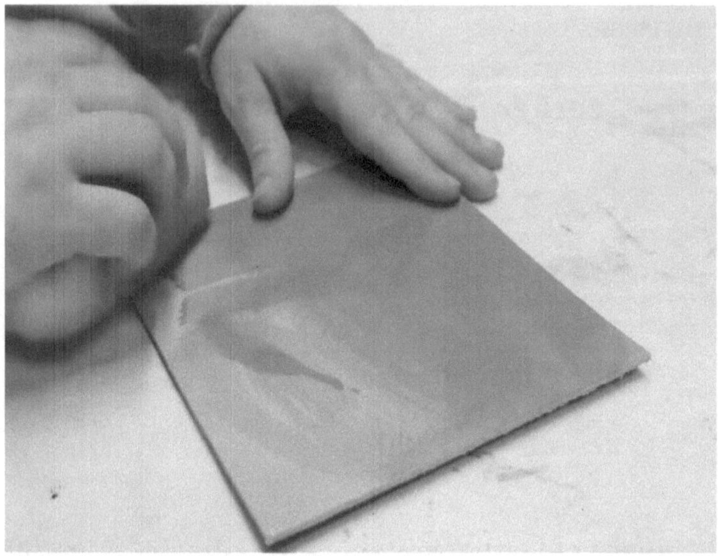

Be cautious not to over-dampen the leather, as excessive moisture can cause the leather to stretch or become distorted. Lightly dampen the leather using a sponge or spray bottle, ensuring it's uniformly moist without being soaked. It's better to gradually add small amounts of water than risk making the leather too wet.

3. *Trace or Draw the Design*

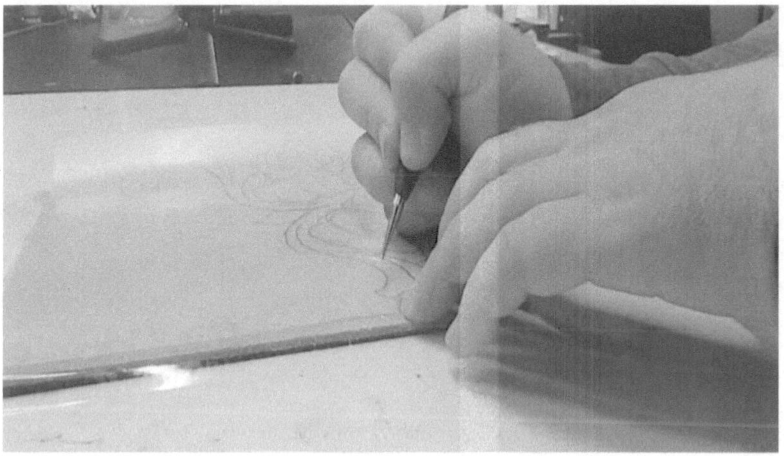

Tracing or drawing your design onto the leather is helpful for a beginner. Use a soft pencil or a stylus to create light markings. Avoid pressing too hard to prevent visible marks after tooling. As you gain confidence, you can transition to freehand tooling and experiment with more complex designs.

4. Use the Swivel Knife

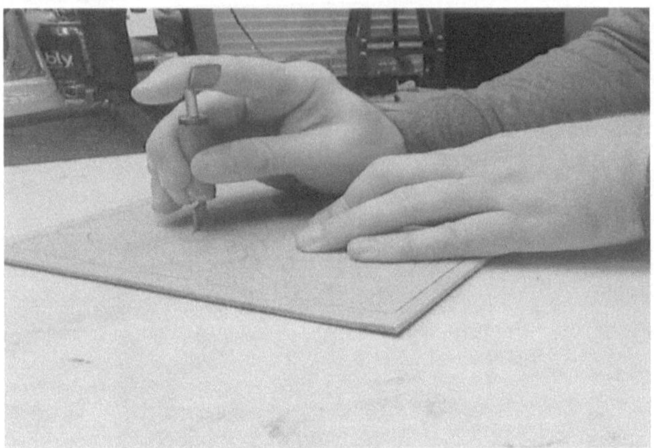

When using the swivel knife, practice on scrap leather first to get a feel for the right amount of pressure and angle. Start with gentle, smooth cuts to avoid cutting too deep into the leather. Gradually increase force as you become more comfortable with the tool.

5. *Emboss the Leather*

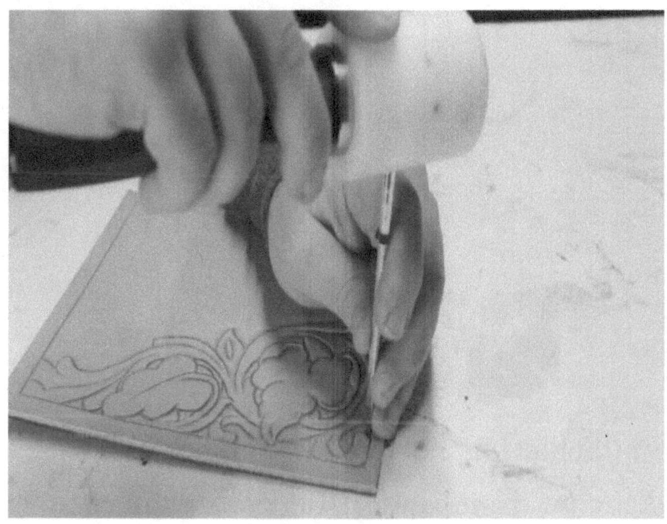

Select a few basic leather tooling stamps with simple designs initially. Practice making impressions on scrap leather to understand how much force is needed. As you progress, experiment with various stamping tools and combinations to create an intricate and captivating design.

6. Work Symmetrically

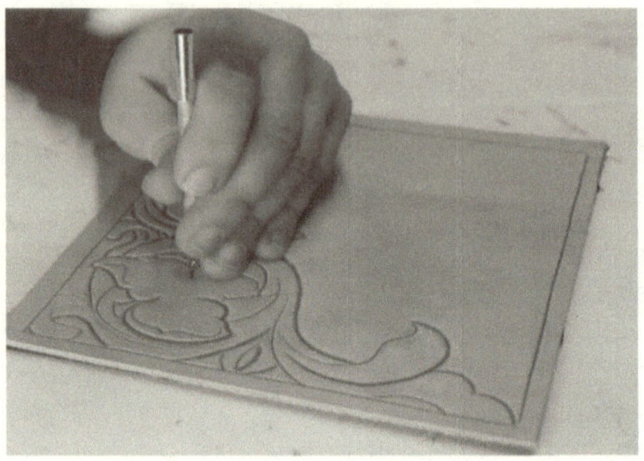

As a beginner, achieving perfect symmetry can be challenging. Take your time and patience, as practice is essential for mastering this skill. Use a ruler or straight edge as a guide to ensure your design elements are evenly spaced and aligned.

7. Create Depth and Texture

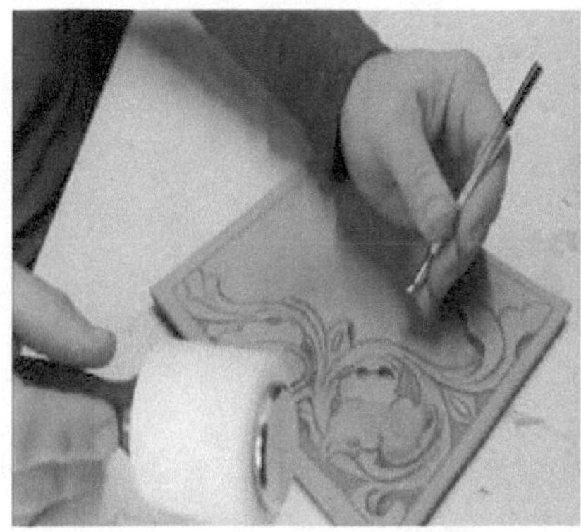
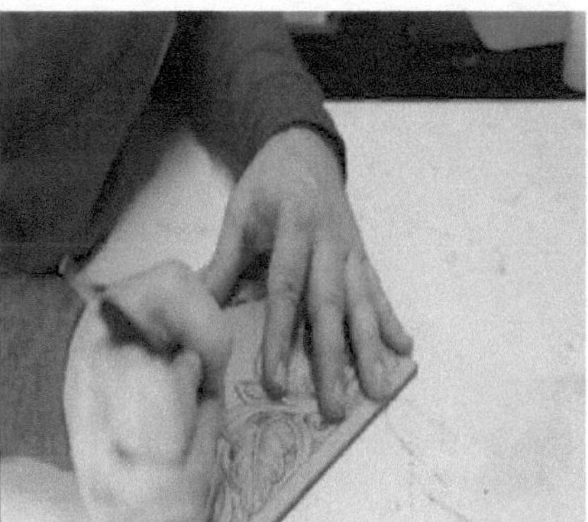

Start with basic beveling techniques to add depth and dimension to your designs. Gradually explore other techniques like veining, seeder stamps, and background stamps to create more intricate textures and visual interest. Don't rush this step; developing a good sense of depth and texture takes practice.

8. Allow the Leather to Dry

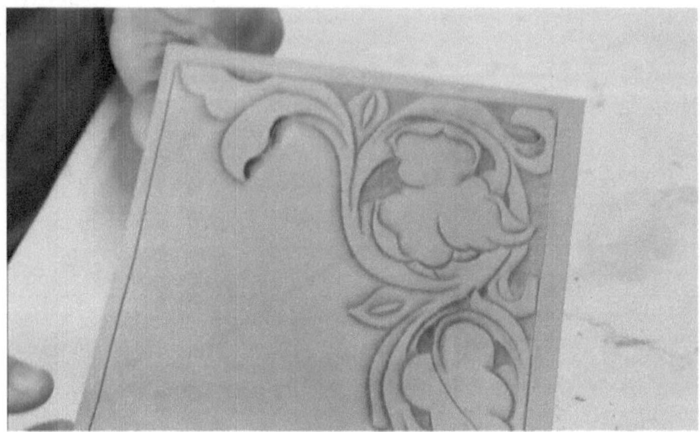

Patience is crucial during the drying process. Allow the leather to air dry naturally to prevent warping. Avoid artificial heat sources like hairdryers, as they can damage the leather.

9. Optional Coloring

Starting with water-based leather dyes is best for a beginner, as they are easier to control and provide consistent results. Practice scrap leather before applying color to your main project to understand how the pigment behaves and how many coats are needed for your desired shade.

10. Finish the Leather

Choose an appropriate finish or conditioner suitable for your project and the type of leather you used. Apply the finish evenly and follow the manufacturer's instructions for best results. Practice on scrap leather to get a sense of the finish's effect before applying it to your finished tooled design.

Remember, leather tooling is an art that requires patience, practice, and creativity. Start with simple designs and gradually challenge yourself with more intricate patterns as your skills improve. Be open to experimenting with different tools and techniques to develop your unique style in leather tooling.

Leather Stamping

Leather stamping is a technique used to create decorative patterns, designs, and textures on the surface of leather using specialized tools called leather stamps. These stamps come in various shapes, sizes, and patterns, allowing leatherworkers to add unique and intricate embellishments to their leather projects.

Leather stamping can be used in a wide range of leatherworking projects, including:

- ***Belts***: Stamping can create beautiful and eye-catching designs on leather belts, adding a personalized touch.
- ***Wallets and Purses***: Leather stamping can embellish the surface of wallets and purses, enhancing their aesthetics and making them more visually appealing.
- ***Holsters and Sheaths***: Leather stamping can be applied to holsters and sheaths to give them a decorative and professional look.
- ***Leather Accessories***: Leather stamping can be used on smaller leather accessories like keychains, wristbands, and phone cases, adding uniqueness and style.
- ***Leather Armor***: In crafting armor pieces or cosplay outfits, leather stamping can create intricate patterns and textures that resemble traditional armor designs.
- ***Leather Covers***: Stamping can be used on leather book covers, journal covers, and notebook covers to give them an artistic and personalized appearance.

- ***Leather Crafts***: Leather stamping is commonly used in various craft projects, such as leather bracelets, earrings, and other artistic pieces.

Leather stamping allows you to showcase your creativity to your leather goods. This versatile technique can be used in functional and decorative leather items, making them unique.

- **Overcoming Challenges During Leather Stamping**

As you begin your journey into leather stamping, you may encounter some challenges. Don't worry; it's all part of the learning process!

Let's explore these common challenges and discover how to overcome them to create beautiful stamped designs on leather.

✓ ***Uneven Impressions***

Getting even impressions can be tricky, but with practice, you'll master it! Make sure to hold the stamp firmly and flat against the leather. Apply consistent pressure throughout the stamping process, and avoid lifting or rocking the symbol—practice on scrap leather to improve your technique and achieve those clean and crisp impressions.

✓ *Misalignment of Designs*

Keeping your designs aligned can be challenging, especially for larger projects. Don't forget to mark the guidelines on the leather before stamping. This will help you maintain alignment and create symmetrical designs. Take your time, plan your layout, and double-check your positioning before each stamp.

✓ *Choosing the Right Stamp*

With so many stamps to choose from, it can feel overwhelming. Start with a basic set of symbols that includes popular shapes and patterns. Experiment with each logo on scrap leather to see how they look and find ones that fit your style.

✓ *Leather Moisture Levels*

The moisture in the leather affects your results. Make sure your leather is lightly damp before stamping. Avoid soaking it; a wet sponge or cloth will do the trick. Keep an eye on the leather's appearance; it should be pliable but not overly wet.

✓ *Depth and Consistency*

Consistent depth in your stamped designs is vital to a professional look. Practice with different pressures on scrap leather until you achieve the desired depth. Maintain a steady hand and even pressure during each stamp. Remember, some stamps need more stress, so adjust your technique accordingly.

✓ ***Over-Stamping***

Accidentally stamping over existing designs can be frustrating, but it happens to all of us! When positioning each stamp, take your time and deliberate your movements. Embrace mistakes as opportunities to improvise or incorporate them into your design.

✓ ***Hand Fatigue***

Leather stamping involves repetitive hand motions, and your hands may get tired. Remember to take short breaks to rest your hands and prevent strain. You can also try using a mallet or stamp handle to reduce effort. With practice, your hands will get used to it, and stamping will become more comfortable.

Embrace these challenges as stepping stones in your leather stamping journey. With determination and practice, you'll develop your skills and create stunning stamped designs that showcase your unique style and creativity. Enjoy the process, and happy stamping!

- **Leather Stamping Process**

Below is the process:

1. *Prepare the Leather*

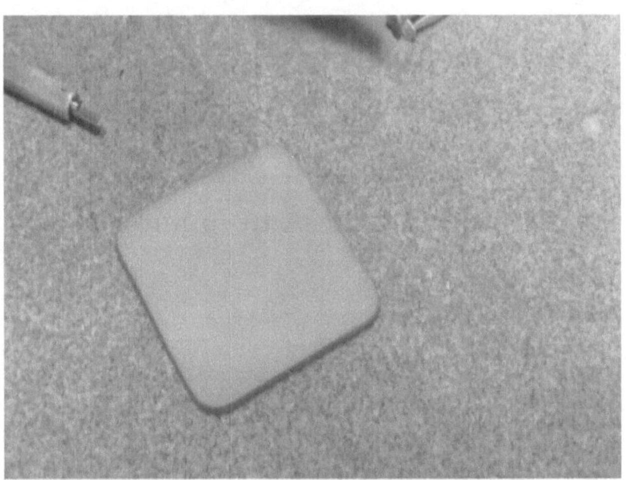

Begin by selecting a piece of leather suitable for stamping. Choose leather with a smooth and firm surface, as it retains impressions well, making it perfect for creating intricate designs. Ensure the leather is clean and free from any blemishes that may affect stamping.

2. *Dampen the Leather*

Before stamping, dampen the leather to make it more pliable and receptive to the stamping tools. Lightly moisten the surface of the leather using a damp sponge, spray bottle, or damp cloth. Avoid over-dampening, as excessive moisture can cause the leather to become too soft or warped.

3. *Trace or Draw the Design*

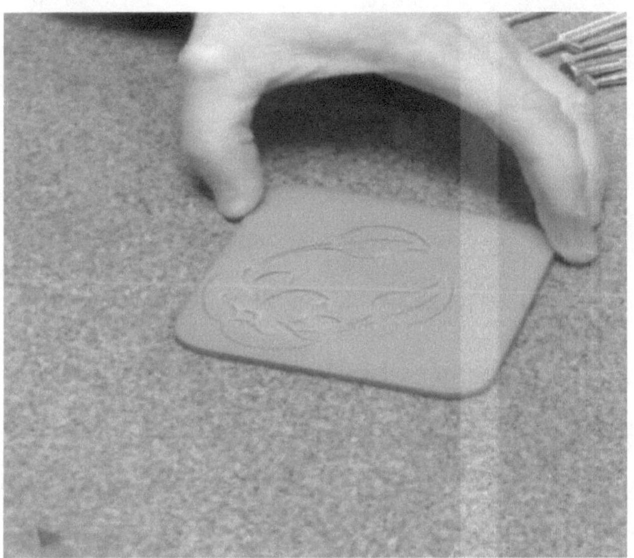

If you have a specific design, you can lightly trace it onto the damp leather using a pencil or stylus. Alternatively, you can freehand the design directly on the leather. As a beginner, tracing can be helpful to guide you and ensure your design is placed correctly.

4. Select the Stamping Tools

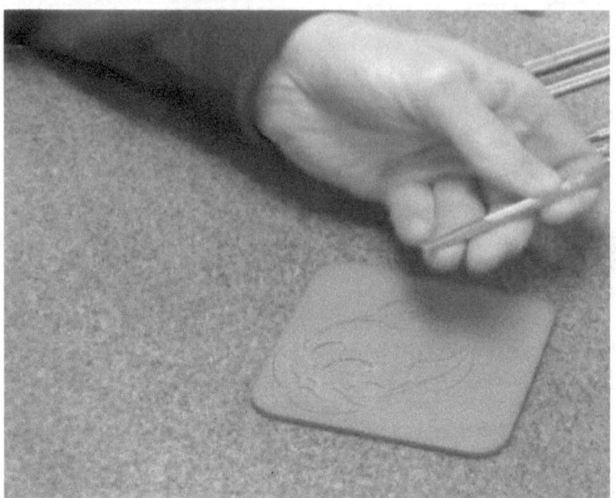

As a beginner, start with a basic set of leather stamping tools. These tools come in various shapes and designs, such as geometric patterns and floral motifs. Choose stamps that you find appealing and align with your creative vision for the project.

5. Position the Stamping Tools

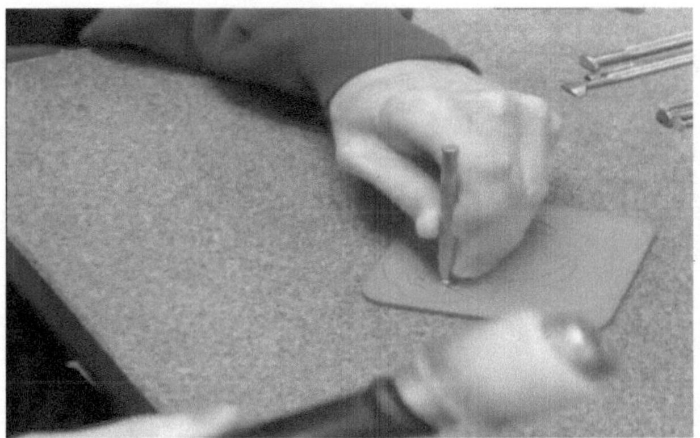

Using a mallet or hammer, strike the stamping tool with firm and even pressure. Aim for one firm strike, as repeatedly hitting the stamp may distort the impression. As a beginner, practice your striking technique on scrap leather to achieve consistent results.

6. Strike the Stamping Tool

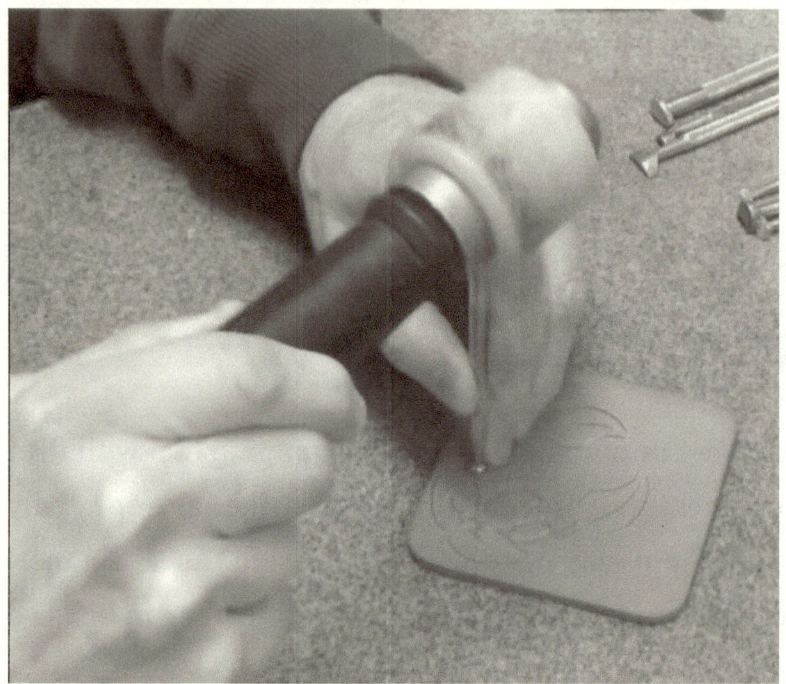

Using a mallet or hammer, strike the stamping tool with firm and even pressure. Aim for one firm strike, as repeatedly hitting the stamp may distort the impression. As a beginner, practice your striking technique on scrap leather to achieve consistent results.

7. Work Symmetrically

As you stamp the leather, try to work symmetrically to maintain balance and consistency in your design. You can repeat the same stamp to create a pattern or combine different stamps for more intricate effects. Take care to place each stamp accurately to create a harmonious overall design.

8. Experiment with Stamping Techniques

Don't be afraid to experiment with different stamping techniques to add depth and texture to your designs. Try using a beveling tool to create raised edges around the stamped design or combine various stamps for layered effects. Remember, practice makes perfect, so experiment on scrap leather to familiarize yourself with different techniques.

9. *Allow the Leather to Dry*

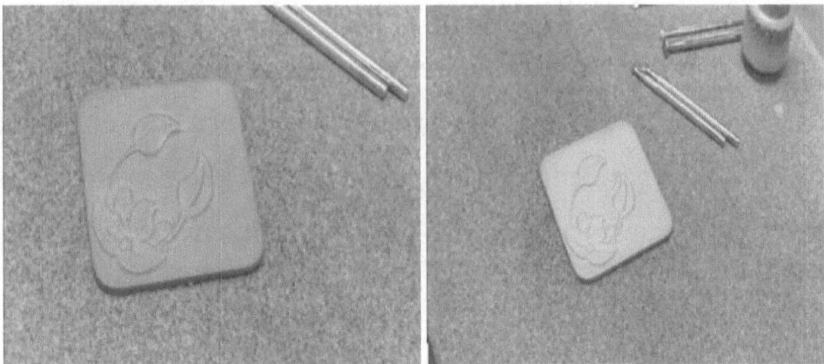

After stamping, allow the leather to dry completely. As the leather dries, the impressions of the stamps will become more pronounced and visually appealing. Resist the temptation to touch or handle the stamped areas until the leather is dehydrated to prevent smudging.

10. *Optional Coloring and Finishing*

If you desire to add color to the stamped design, you can use leather dyes, stains, or finishes. Applying color to the stamped leather enhances the overall visual appeal and brings the design to life. Choose colors that complement your project and apply them evenly for a polished finish. Once the coloring is complete (if applied), finish the leather using appropriate leather finishes or conditioners to protect and preserve the stamped design.

As a beginner, take your time with each step of the stamping process—practice on scrap leather to improve your skills and gain confidence before working on your main project. With dedication and patience, you'll develop your unique style in leather stamping and create stunning and personalized leather pieces. Enjoy the journey of exploring this beautiful craft!

Chapter 7: Step 4-Dyeing and Finishing

Dyeing and finishing add color, depth, and protection to leather—Let's explore the dyeing and finishing process, as well as techniques for achieving desired effects.

Dyeing

Dyeing is the process of applying color to the surface of the leather to achieve the desired hue or shade. Leather dye is a coloring agent that penetrates the leather fibers, creating a long-lasting and vibrant coloration. Dyeing is an essential technique in leatherworking that allows artisans to add personalization, style, and visual appeal to their leather projects.

- **When Dyeing is Used**

Dyeing is used in various leatherworking projects to achieve specific design goals and enhance the overall aesthetics of the leather.

Some common instances when dyeing is used include:

✓ ***Customization:*** Dyeing allows leatherworkers to customize their projects with unique colors, creating unique pieces that reflect their style or suit a client's preferences.

- ✓ ***Restoring and Reviving Leather*:** Dyeing is often employed to refresh and repair old or faded leather items. It can bring new life to worn-out leather goods, making them look fresh and presentable.

- ✓ ***Creating Patterns and Designs*:** Leather dye can create intricate patterns and designs on the leather's surface. Leatherworkers can produce visually striking and artistic effects by applying the dye selectively or using various techniques like marbling, splattering, or gradient dyeing.

- ✓ ***Color Matching*:** When working on leather projects that require matching specific colors, dyeing is the go-to method. You can adjust the dye's concentration and apply multiple layers to achieve the desired color tone.

- ✓ ***Leather Crafting Projects***: Dyeing is widely used in crafting leather goods such as belts, wallets, handbags, shoes, and small leather accessories. It allows artisans to elevate their products' appearance and offer customers diverse colors.

- ✓ ***Leather Artwork*:** Leather artists and artisans often use dyeing as a primary medium to create beautiful and intricate artworks on leather canvases.

It's important to note that the type of leather dye used can impact the final result. Different leather dyes are available, including alcohol-based, water-based, and oil-based dyes, each with unique characteristics. You should choose the appropriate dye based on your project's requirements and the desired finish.

- **Factors To Consider When Selecting The Suitable Leather Dye For Your Project**

✓ ***Project Requirements***: Assess the type of leather you are working with and the specific requirements of your project. Some dyes work better on certain types of leather than others. For example, water-based dyes are suitable for vegetable-tanned leather, while alcohol-based dyes are better for chrome-tanned leather. Understanding the compatibility between the dye and your leather type is essential for achieving the best results.

✓ ***Desired Finish***: Different dyes can produce varying effects on leather. Alcohol-based dyes often provide a more intense and vibrant color, while water-based dyes offer a softer and more subtle hue. Oil-based dyes can create a rich and deep color with a glossy finish. Consider the look and feel you want to achieve and choose a dye that aligns with your artistic vision.

- ✓ ***Ease of Application***: Some dyes may be easier to apply than others. Water-based dyes are generally more forgiving and easier to control during application, making them a good choice for beginners. On the other hand, alcohol-based dyes may require more precision and experience to achieve an even color distribution.
- ✓ ***Dye Permanence***: Consider the durability and permanence of the dye. Some dyes penetrate deeper into the leather and offer better colorfastness, ensuring your project maintains its vibrant look for an extended period.
- ✓ ***Environmental Considerations***: Water-based dyes are generally considered more eco-friendly and easier to clean up, as they use water as the solvent. If ecological impact concerns you, this might be a factor to consider.

Ultimately, experimentation and practice will help you become more familiar with different types of dyes and their effects. Before applying them to your main project, don't hesitate to test dyes on small leather swatches. This way, you can make an informed decision and achieve the desired results in your leatherworking endeavors.

Overall, dyeing is a versatile and essential technique in leatherworking, offering endless possibilities for creating visually stunning and personalized leather products. As a leatherworker, understanding the various dyeing techniques and mastering the application process will enhance your leather projects' quality and artistic appeal.

- **Overcoming challenges during Leather Dyeing**

As a beginner in leather dyeing, you may encounter some challenges, but with practice and patience, you can overcome them and achieve beautiful results.

Here are some common challenges and tips to overcome them:

✓ ***Uneven Dye Application*:** One of the most common challenges is achieving an even dye application on the leather surface. Uneven dyeing can result in blotchy or streaky colors.

✓ To overcome this, thoroughly ***clean and prepare*** the leather surface before dying. Remove any dirt, oils, or previous finishes to ensure the dye can penetrate evenly.

✓ ***Apply the dye in thin, even layers using a sponge or applicator***. Avoid applying too much dye in one area, leading to uneven results. Allow each layer to dry before adding another coat.

- ✓ ***Color Darkening or Lightening*:** Dye color may appear darker or lighter than expected on the leather, which can be challenging to predict.
- ✓ ***Test the dye on a small, inconspicuous leather area*** before applying it to the project. This will help you gauge how the color will look once it dries.
- ✓ Remember that the dye's color may change as it dries and interacts with the leather. ***Allow the dye to dry fully before assessing the final color***.
- ✓ ***Dye Bleeding*:** Sometimes, the dye may bleed or spread beyond the intended area, especially on porous or untreated leather.
- ✓ ***Use a resist agent or edge paint*** to create boundaries and prevent the dye from bleeding into unwanted areas.
- ✓ ***Apply the dye with care***, ensuring not to oversaturate the leather, which can cause bleeding.
- ✓ **Achieving Consistent Color:** Getting consistent color across the entire project can be challenging, particularly when dyeing large surfaces or multiple pieces.
- ✓ ***Mix sufficient dye*** and ensure consistency throughout the project to maintain uniform color.

- ✓ ***Apply the dye in the same manner and pressure*** to all areas for consistent results.
- ✓ ***Staining Hands and Workspace*:** Dye can stain your hands and the surrounding workspace if not handled carefully.
- ✓ ***Wear gloves to protect your hands from staining***. Disposable nitrile gloves are suitable for this purpose.
- ✓ ***Cover your workspace with newspapers or plastic*** to prevent dye from staining the surface. Clean up any spills or splatters immediately.
- ✓ ***Dyeing in Hard-to-Reach Areas*:** Some projects may have intricate details or hard-to-reach areas that are challenging to dye evenly.
- ✓ ***Use cotton swabs or small brushes*** to apply the dye in tight spaces or intricate designs.
- ✓ ***Take your time and work carefully*** to ensure even dye coverage in difficult areas.

Remember that leather dyeing is a skill that improves with practice. Don't be discouraged by initial challenges. Instead, embrace them as learning opportunities and continue to experiment with different techniques and dyes. As you gain experience, you'll become more confident in your abilities and achieve outstanding results in your leather dyeing projects.

- **The Dyeing Process**

1. *Prepare the Leather*

Before dying, ensure the leather surface is clean and free from dirt, oil, or previous finishes. You can use a soft cloth or leather cleaner to wipe the leather and remove any surface contaminants gently. If there are blemishes or stains, consider sanding the leather lightly to create a smooth and even surface for dye application. Dampening the leather can help improve dye penetration, especially for vegetable-tanned leather.

2. *Test the Dye*

Testing the dye on a small, inconspicuous leather area is crucial before applying it to the entire project. This test will give you an idea of how the color will look and how the leather reacts to the dye. Apply a small amount of dye with your applicator and allow it to dry completely. Assess the color and ensure it matches your desired outcome before proceeding.

3. *Wear Protective Gloves*

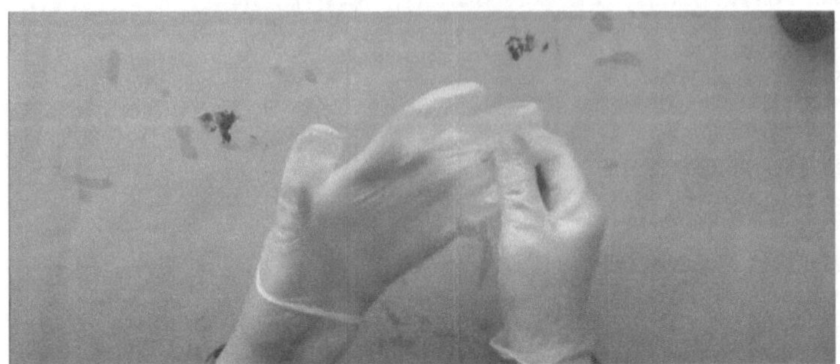

Always wear protective gloves when handling leather dye to prevent staining your hands and avoid potential skin irritation. Nitrile gloves are suitable for this purpose, as they offer good protection and allow for talent while working with the dye.

4. *Apply the Dye*

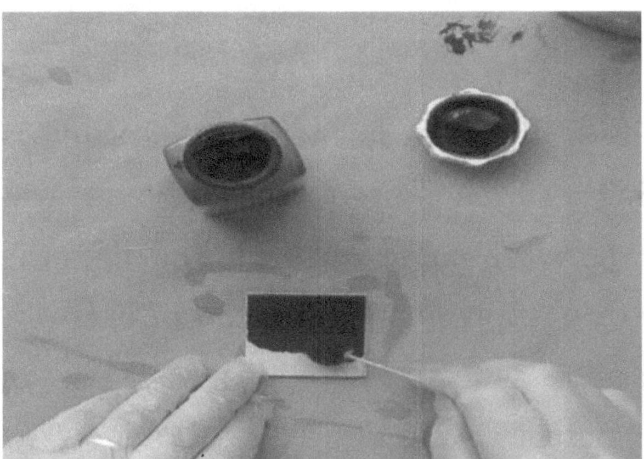

Shake the dye bottle well to ensure it's properly mixed. Dip your applicator (sponge, wool dauber, or brush) into the dye, and apply it to the leather in even strokes. Begin in small sections, working your way across the project. Use a light touch to control the color intensity, and avoid oversaturating the leather, as this can lead to uneven results.

5. Allow the Dye to Dry

After dyeing the leather, allow it to dry completely. The drying time will vary depending on the type of dye used and the environmental conditions. Avoid touching the leather while drying to prevent smudging or uneven coloring.

6. Apply Additional Coats (Optional)

If you desire a darker or more intense color, apply additional coats of dye after the first one has dried. Be patient and allow each coat to dry completely before adding more layers. Multiple thin coats are preferable to avoid overloading the leather with dye.

7. Buff the Leather

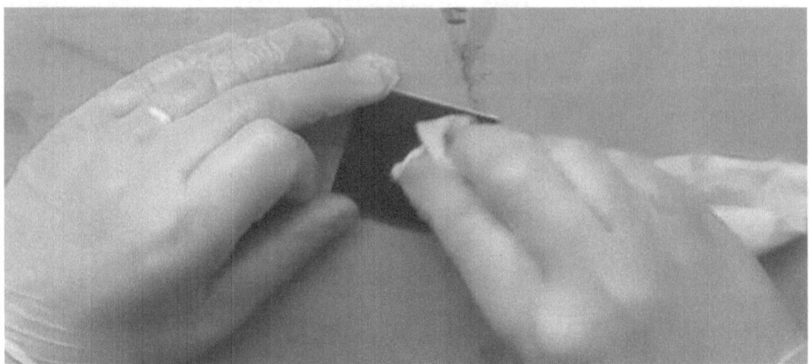

Once the dye has dried, you can buff the leather with a soft cloth or rag to enhance its shine and smoothness. This step is optional and can add a polished look to the dyed leather.

8. Enjoy Your Dyed Leather

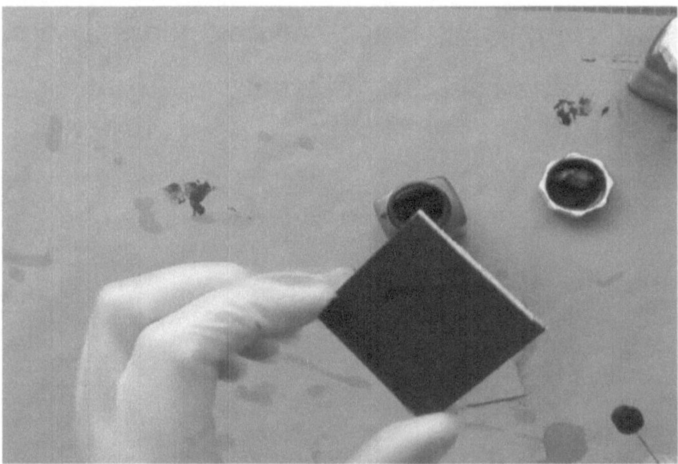

Your leather is dyed and ready for various projects such as belts, wallets, bags, etc. Keep in mind that leather dyeing is a skill that improves with practice. Start with simple tasks and experiment with different dye colors to develop your style.

- **Leather Dyeing Techniques**

Leather dyeing techniques are essential skills for any leatherworker. These techniques allow you to add color, depth, and character to your leather projects.

Here are some popular leather dyeing techniques:

✓ ***Solid Dyeing***

Solid dyeing is the most foundational and straightforward leather dyeing technique. It involves applying a single, even layer of dye to the entire leather surface, resulting in a consistent and uniform color. This technique creates classic leather goods like belts, wallets, small accessories, and oversized items like sheaths or leather covers. Solid dyeing allows you to achieve a clean and polished look, making it an essential skill for any leatherworker.

To Apply The Dye:

Step 1:

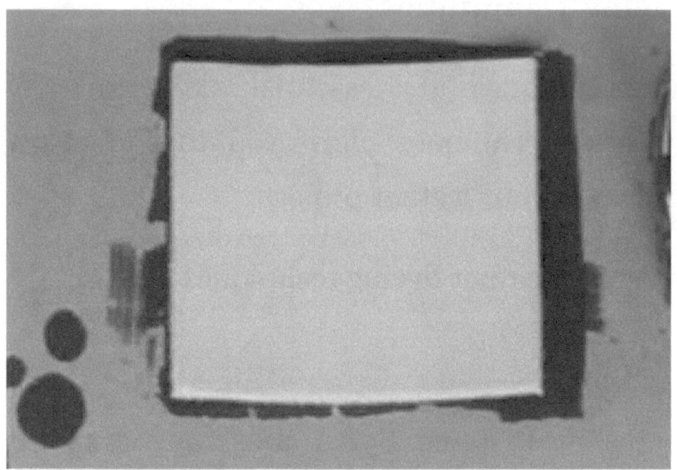

Prepare the leather: Ensure the leather surface is clean and free from dirt or debris.

Step 2:

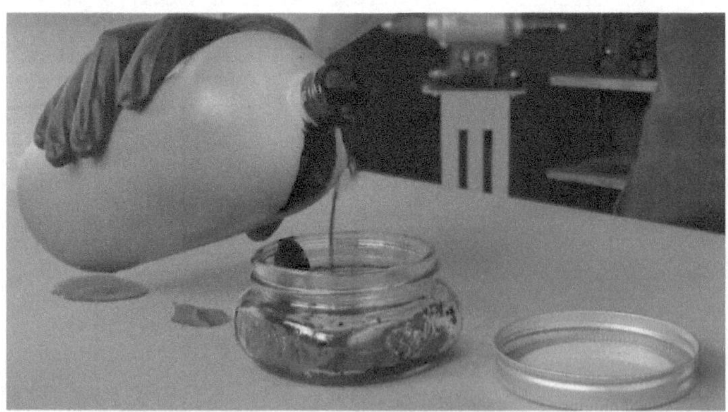

Choose the dye: Select a suitable dye color for your project. Make sure it complements the leather and achieves the desired look.

Step 3:

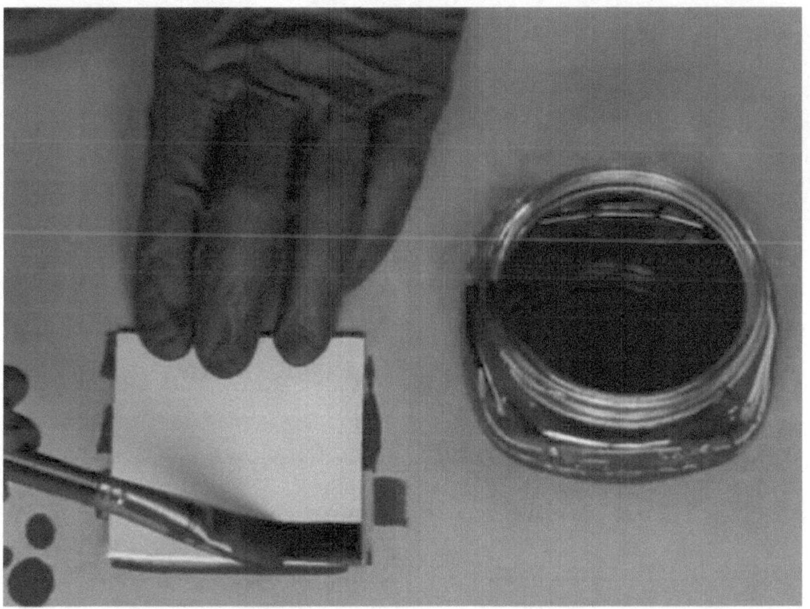

Apply the dye: Use a sponge, brush, or airbrush to apply the dye in even and thin layers to the entire leather surface.

Step 4: Let it dry: Allow each layer of dye to dry before adding the next to avoid streaks or blotches

Step 5:

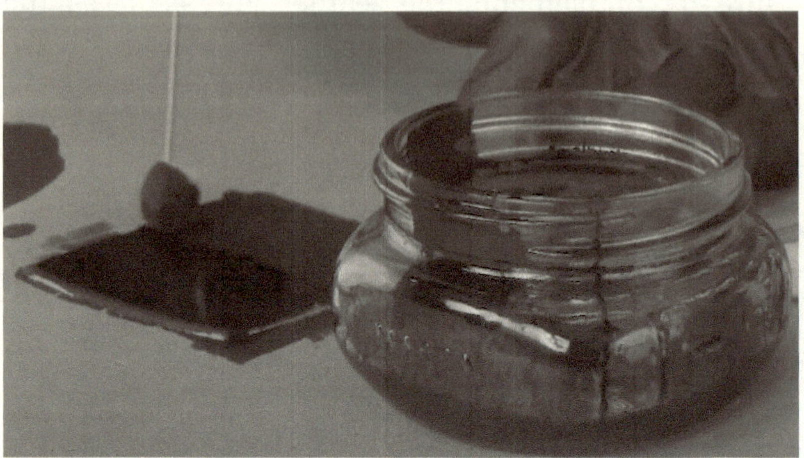

Repeat if necessary: If you want a deeper color, repeat the dyeing process until you achieve the desired shade.

This technique lays the foundation for more advanced dyeing methods, and mastering solid dyeing is essential before exploring other techniques.

✓ ***Antiquing***

Antiquing, also known as ***staining***, is a technique that adds depth and character to leather by darkening specific areas such as edges, seams, and creases, creating an aged and weathered appearance. This technique is perfect for achieving a vintage and time-worn look in your leather projects. Antiquing works wonders for making vintage-style belts, leather journals, pouches, and other accessories that benefit from a rustic and timeless charm.

To Apply The Dye:

Step 1:

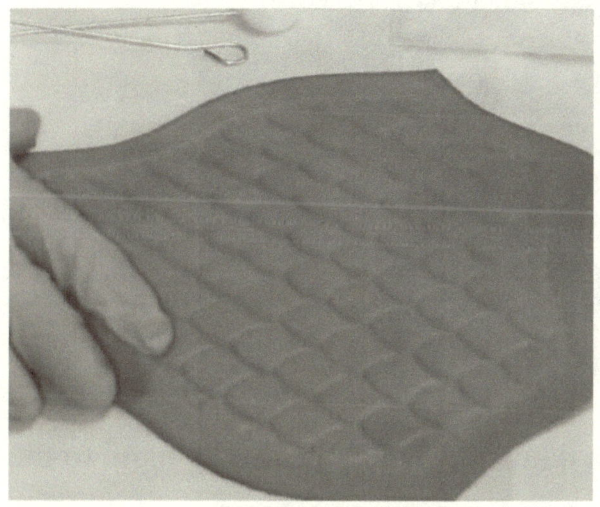

Identify areas to darken: Decide which parts of the leather you want to give an aged appearance, such as edges, seams, and creases.

Step 2: Choose the antiquing dye: Select a darker dye shade to create the antiquing effect.

Step 3:

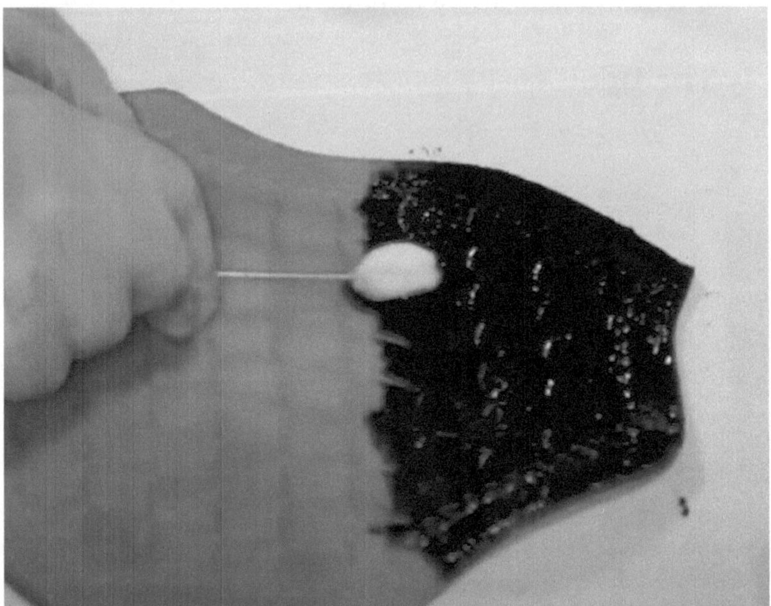

Apply the dye: Use a dauber or apply the dye by hand to the desired areas, focusing on the edges and creases.

Step 4: Blend the dye: Use a cloth or sponge to gradually transition between the antiqued areas and the rest of the leather.

Step 5:

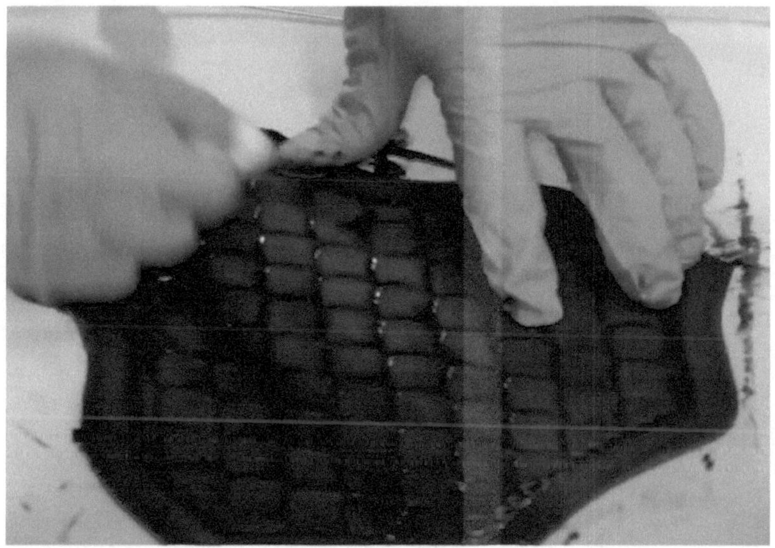

Wipe off excess dye: After applying the dye, wipe away any excess to achieve the desired weathered effect.

The key to successful antiquing is to apply the dye selectively and purposefully, emphasizing the areas that would naturally age and darken over time.

Ombre Dyeing

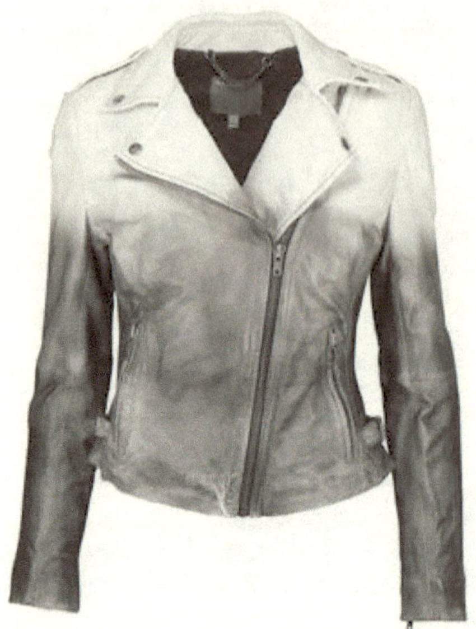

Ombre dyeing is a captivating technique that smoothly creates a beautiful gradient effect, transitioning from one color to another. This technique adds a touch of artistry and sophistication to your leather projects, making it a popular choice for items like bags, wallets, and decorative leather accents.

To Achieve The Ombre Effect:

Step 1:

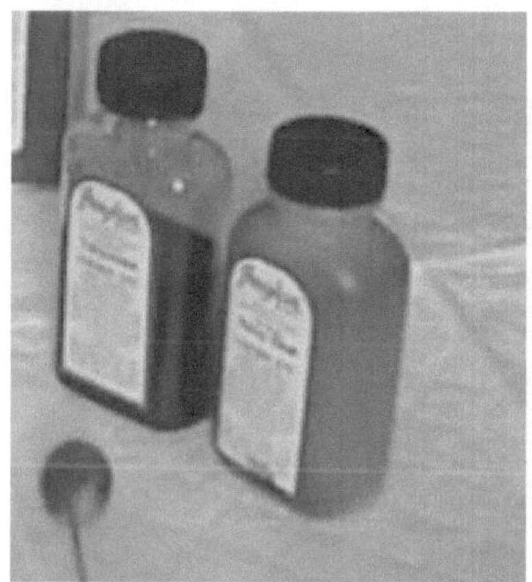

Select dye colors: Choose two or more colors that blend well together for the ombre effect.

Step 2:

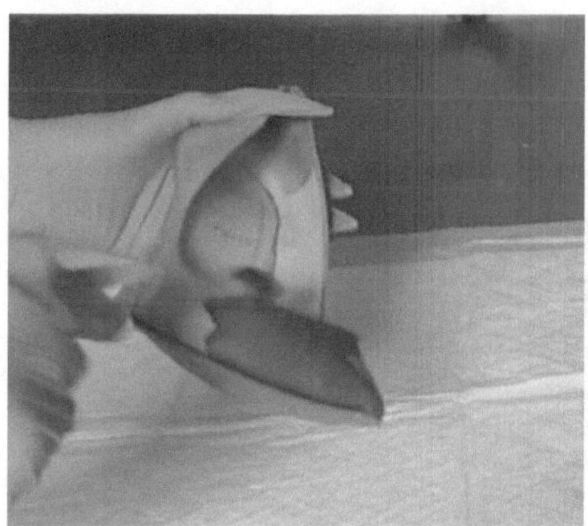

Apply the lightest color: Apply the lighter color to one end of the leather.

Step 3:

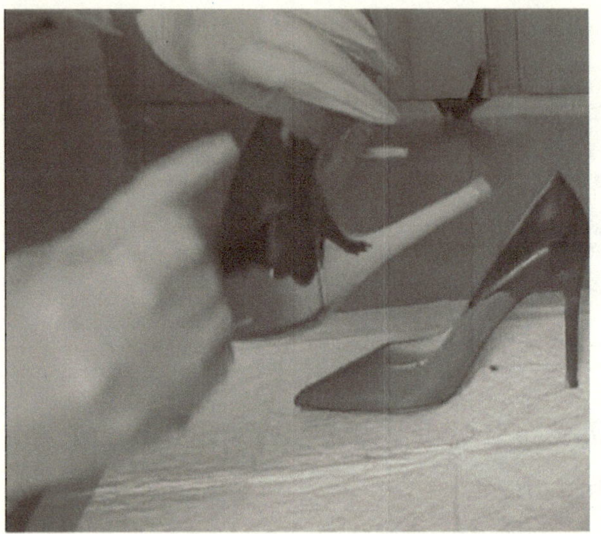

Apply the darkest color: Apply the darker color to the other end of the leather.

Step 4:

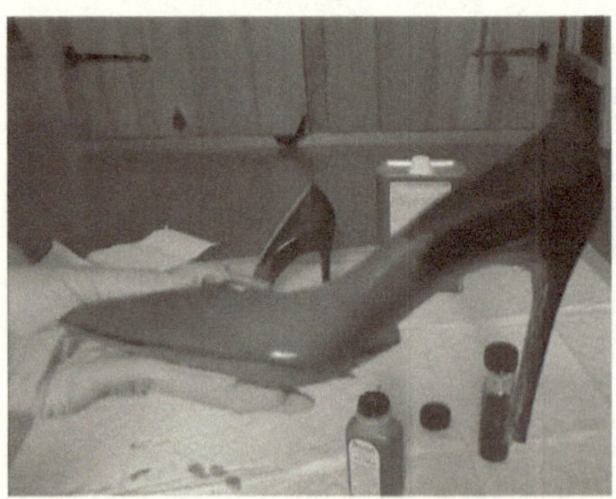

Blend the colors: Using a sponge or brush to blend the colors in the middle creates a smooth transition.

Experiment with different blending techniques: Practice blending the colors differently to achieve various ombre effects. This technique requires practice and precision to perform the desired gradient smoothly.

✓ ***Two-Tone Dyeing***

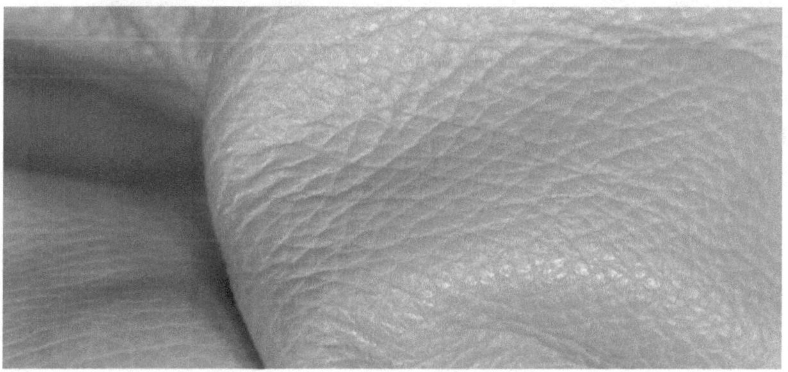

Two-tone dyeing is a versatile technique using two colors to contrast and highlight specific leather parts. This technique allows you to add visual interest and complexity to your designs, making them suitable for belts, watch straps, wallets, and any leather project with distinct areas.

To Apply The Dye:

Step 1:

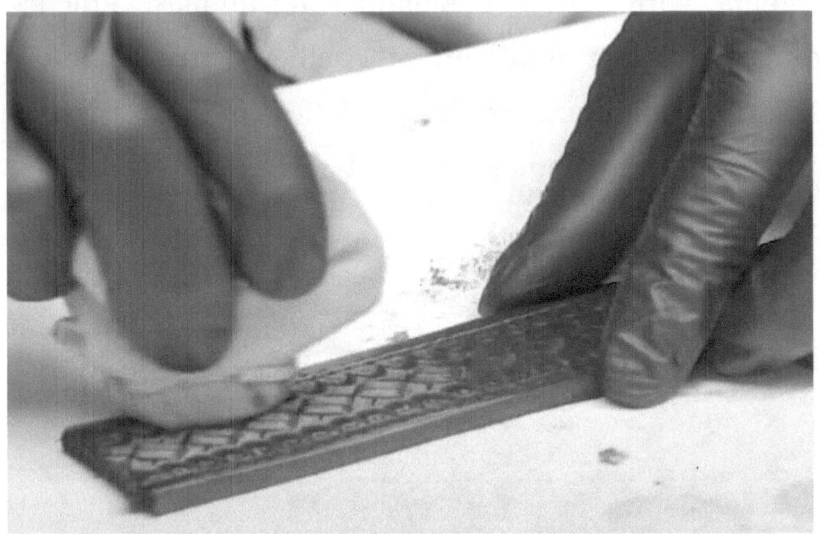

Cover the leather with one color: Start by dyeing the entire leather surface with one color.

Step 2: Mask off areas: Once dry, mask off the areas you want to remain the first color.

Step 3: Apply the second color: Apply the second color to the exposed sections, making sure to achieve clean and well-defined color transitions.

Step 4: Blend if necessary: Use a sponge or brush to blend the colors if a gradual transition is desired.

This technique requires careful planning and execution to ensure clean, well-defined color transitions. Consider using complementary or contrasting colors to create a striking visual impact in your two-tone dyeing projects.

✓ ***Faux Patina***

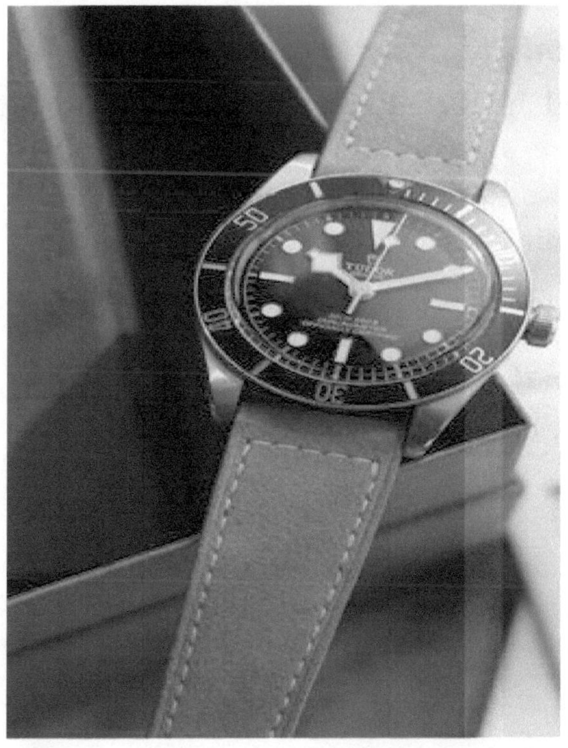

A faux patina is a skillful technique replicating the natural aging and patina development found in well-worn leather items. This technique is perfect for achieving a vintage and aged appearance on leather bags, shoes, and accessories.

To Create The Faux Patina:

1. ***Prepare the leather***: Ensure the leather is clean and ready for dyeing.

2. Layer the dyes: Apply multiple layers of dye in various shades to create depth and richness.

3. ***Darken edges and high-wear areas***: Use darker colors on edges and areas that naturally age and darken over time.

4. ***Add texture***: Use finishes and stains to add texture and create a weathered look.

5. ***Emphasize natural aging***: Pay attention to the areas that would naturally develop.

Faux patina requires careful layering and blending of colors to achieve an authentic and natural-looking aged effect.

✓ *Marbling*

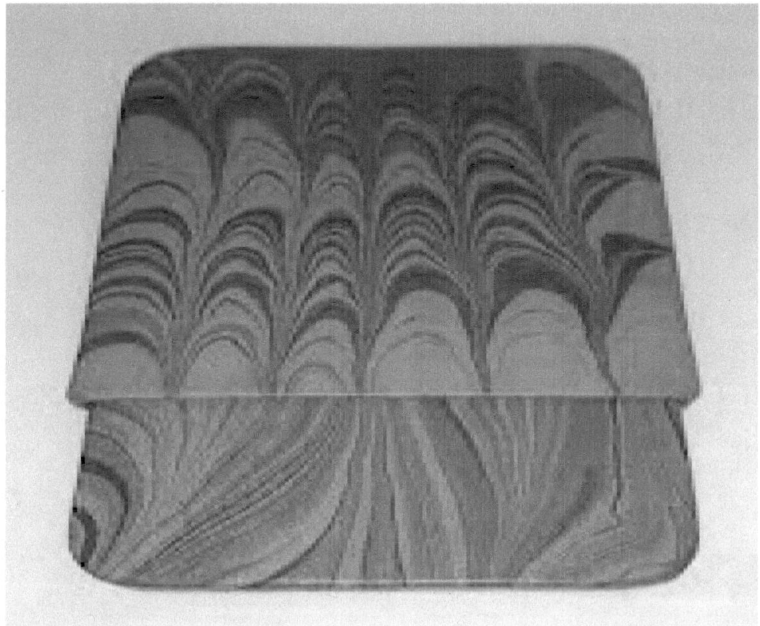

Marbling is a unique and artistic technique that involves swirling and blending different colors on the leather surface to create a marbled pattern. This technique is commonly used to add elegance and visual intrigue to book covers, journals, and statement leather accessories.

To Apply The Dye:

Step 1:

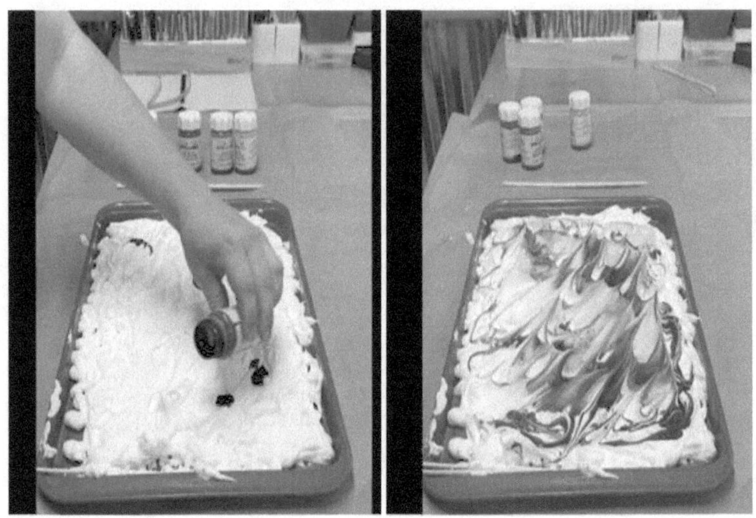

Drop or pour different colored dyes: Drop or pour other colored dyes into the leather surface.

Step 2:

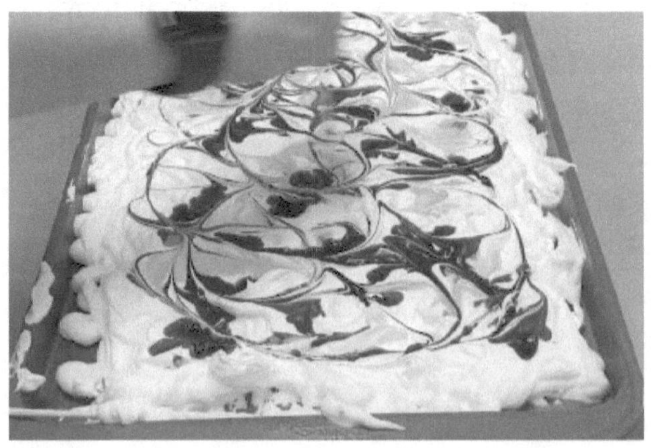

Create swirling patterns: Use a comb, needle, or stylus to create swirling patterns with the dyes.

Step 3:

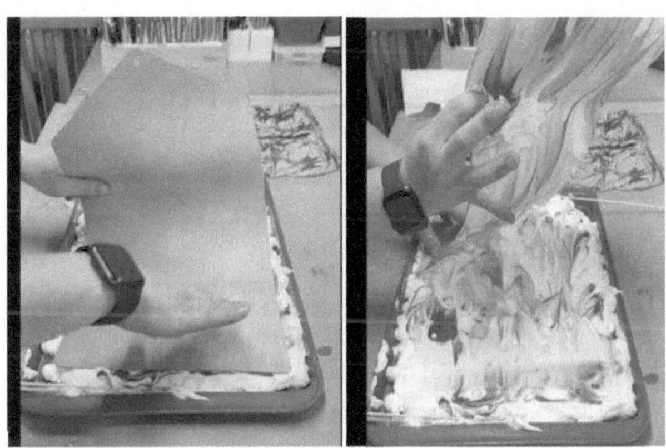

Experiment with color combinations: Try different combinations to create visually captivating marbled designs.

- ✓ ***Slattering***

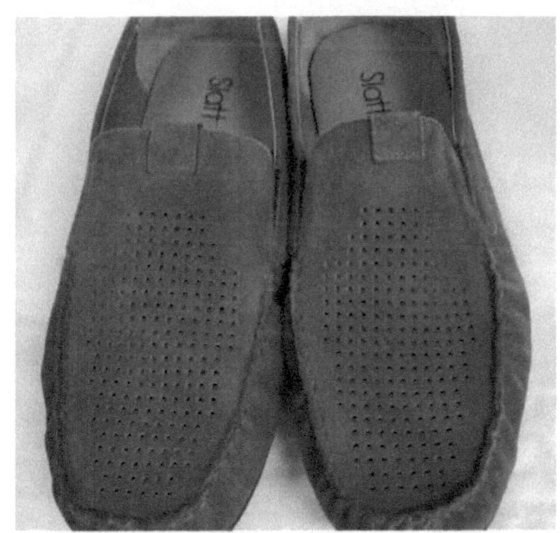

Splattering is a fun and spontaneous dyeing technique that adds a unique and expressive touch to leather projects.

To Achieve The Splatter Effect:

1. ***Prepare the Leather***: Choose a clean and prepped leather piece for splattering. Make sure it is free from any dust or dirt.

2. ***Wear Protective Gear***: Wear protective gloves to prevent staining your hands during splattering. It's also a good idea to work in a well-ventilated area or wear a mask if you are using an airbrush.

3. ***Choose the Colors***:

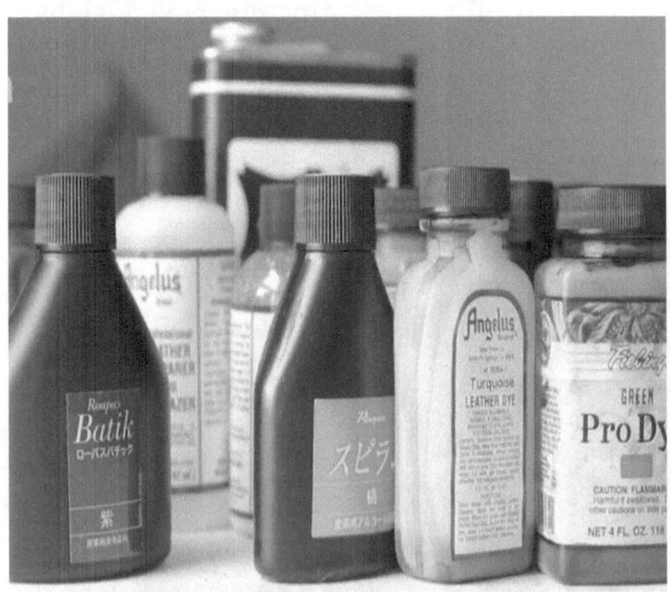

Select the leather dye colors you want to use for the splattering effect. You can use one color for a monochromatic look or multiple colors for a more vibrant and colorful design.

4. ***Dilute the Dye*** (Optional): If your leather dye is highly concentrated, you may choose to dilute it with water to achieve a lighter and more transparent splattering effect. Test the dye on a scrap piece of leather to determine the desired concentration level.

5. ***Prepare the Brushes or Airbrush***: Dip the bristles into the dye if you're using brushes. If you're using an airbrush, load the airbrush with the diluted dye according to the manufacturer's instructions.

6. ***Splatter the Dye***: Hold the brush or airbrush a few inches above the leather surface to splatter the dye onto the leather. Use your fingers to flick the bristles or press the airbrush trigger to release the dye in quick and controlled bursts. The dye will create random speckles and droplets on the leather.

7. ***Experiment with Techniques:*** You can vary the intensity of the splattering by adjusting the distance between the brush or airbrush and the leather surface.

Experiment with different flicking or spraying techniques to achieve the desired splatter pattern.

8. ***Layer the Colors (Optional):*** If using multiple colors, allow the first color to dry before adding additional colors. Layering different shades of splatter can create exciting and dynamic effects.

9. ***Let the Dye Set***: Allow the leather dye to set and penetrate the leather. Follow the recommended dye manufacturer's instructions for the specific setting time.

10. ***Rinse or Heat-Set*** (Optional): Depending on the type of leather dye used, you may need to rinse off any excess dye after the setting time has passed. Alternatively, some dyes may require heat-setting by using a heat gun or iron. Follow the dye manufacturer's guidelines for the appropriate method.

11. ***Let It Dry***: Lay the splattered leather piece flat and allow it to dry completely. Avoid folding or manipulating the leather while drying to maintain the random splatter pattern.

12. ***Finish and Protect*** (Optional): Apply a leather finish or conditioner to protect and enhance the splattered design once the leather is dry. Follow the instructions on the leather finish product for proper application.

Splattering is an excellent technique for adding texture and creating a sense of movement in your leather creations.

✓ ***Gradient Dyeing***

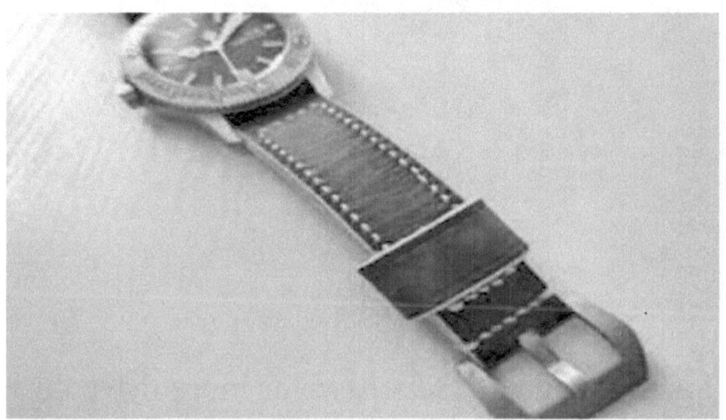

Gradient dyeing, also known as ***shading or fading***, involves creating a smooth transition of color from one shade to another. This technique is used to achieve subtle and gradual changes in color intensity across the leather surface.

To Achieve The Gradient Effect:

Step 1:

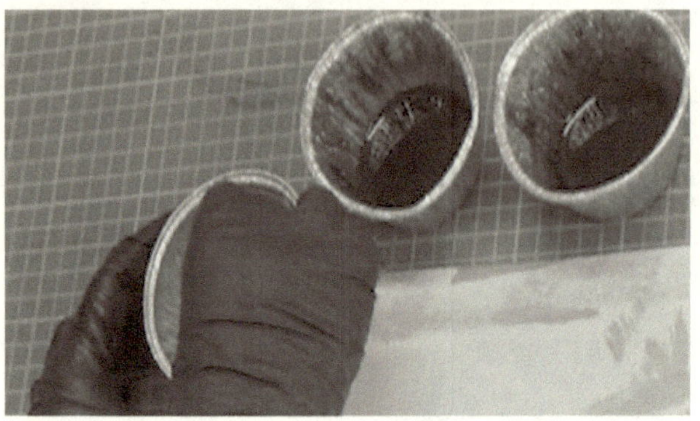

Choose colors for the gradient: Select two or more dye colors that blend well.

Step 2:

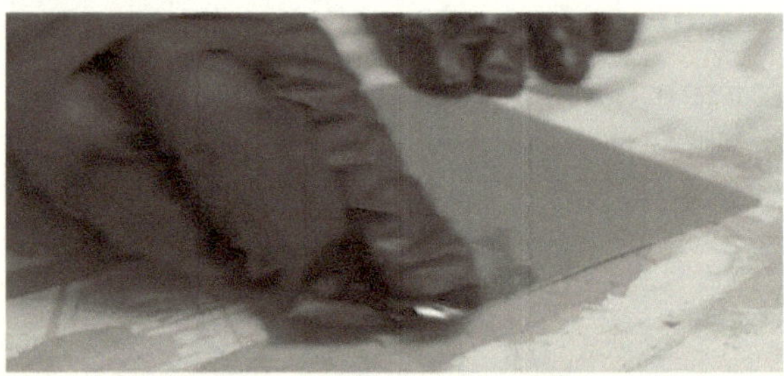

Apply the concentrated dye: Start by applying the dye in a concentrated form on one end of the leather.

Step 3:

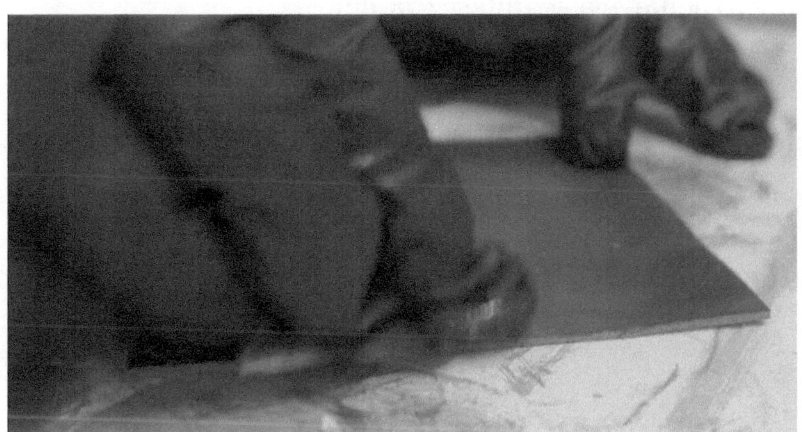

Gradually dilute the dye: Use a wet sponge or brush to gradually dilute the dye as you move towards the other end.

Step 4:

Blend carefully: Take your time and blend the colors smoothly to achieve a seamless gradient.

Gradient dyeing is often used to create realistic color gradients, such as in nature-inspired designs or realistic portrayals of landscapes.

✓ ***Color Blocking***

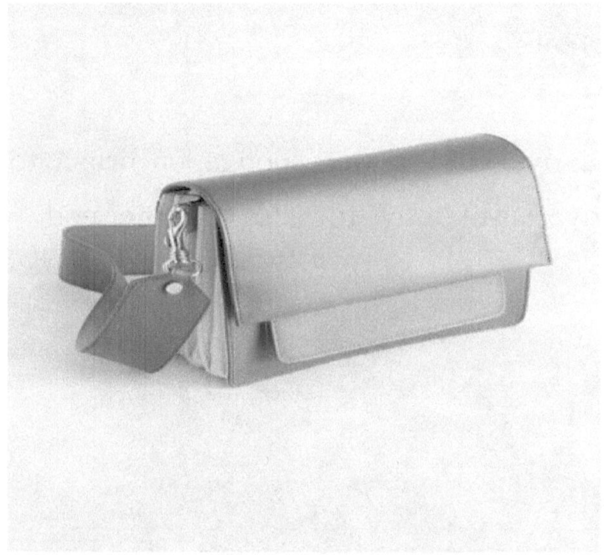

Color blocking is a bold and modern technique that uses contrasting colors to create well-defined blocks of color on the leather. This technique allows you to create contemporary and eye-catching designs on bags, wallets, and modern leather apparel.

To Apply The Dye:

Step 1:

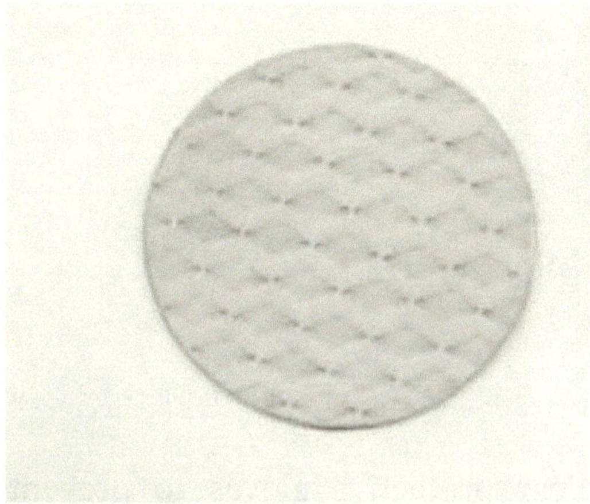

Prepare the Leather: Choose a clean, prepped leather piece for color blocking. Make sure it is free from any dust or dirt.

Step 2: Mask Off Areas (Optional): If you want to maintain one color while applying the other color to specific sections, mask off the areas you wish to remain the first color. You can use masking tape or any other material to create clean edges.

Step 3:

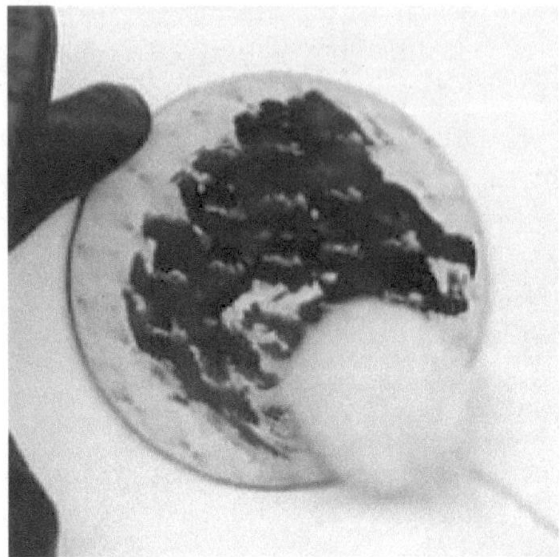

Apply the First Color: Wear protective gloves to prevent staining your hands. Using a sponge or brush, apply the first color of leather dye to the exposed areas of the leather. Apply the dye evenly and generously to ensure complete coverage.

Step 4:

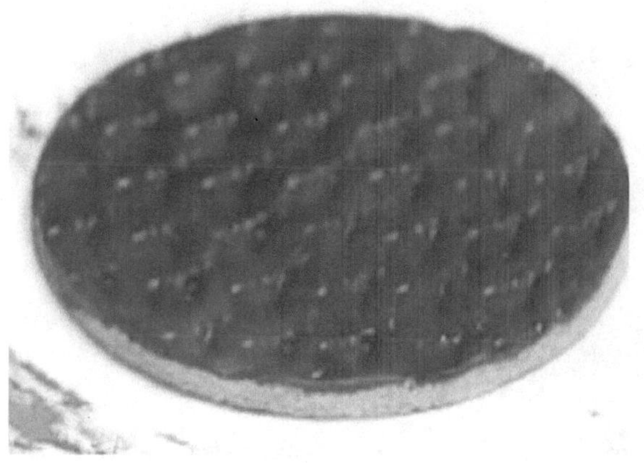

Let the First Color Dry: The first dye color dries completely. Follow the recommended dye manufacturer's instructions for drying time.

Step 5: Mask Off Different Areas (Optional): If you want to create multiple blocks of different colors, mask off the areas or the next color. Ensure that the masking material is firmly secured to prevent bleeding of colors.

Step 6:

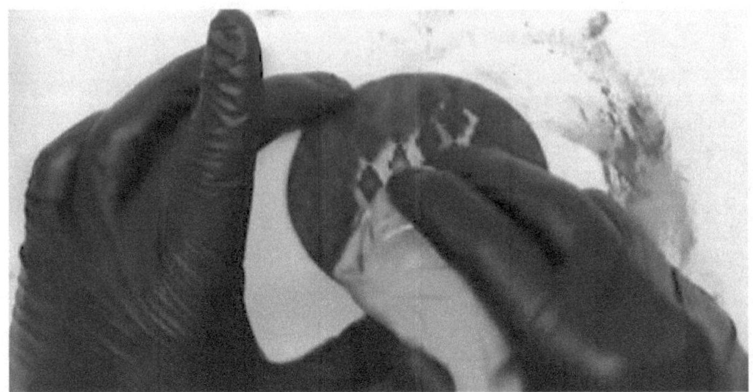

Apply the Second Color: Once the first color is dry, apply the second color of leather dye to the designated areas. Again, use a sponge or brush to apply the dye evenly and avoid streaks or blotches.

Step 7: Blend the Colors (Optional): If you want a clean transition between the color blocks, you can use a sponge or brush to blend the colors where they meet. This will create a smooth and seamless transition between the two colors.

Step 8: Remove the Masking Material (If Used): If you used masking tape or other materials to create clean edges between color blocks, carefully remove them once the dye has dried.

Step 9: Let the Dye Set: Allow the leather dye to set and penetrate the leather. Follow the recommended dye manufacturer's instructions for the specific setting time.

Step 10: Rinse or Heat-Set (Optional): Depending on the type of leather dye used, you may need to rinse off any excess dye after the setting time has passed. Alternatively, some dyes may require heat-setting by using a heat gun or iron. Follow the dye manufacturer's guidelines for the appropriate method.

Step 11:

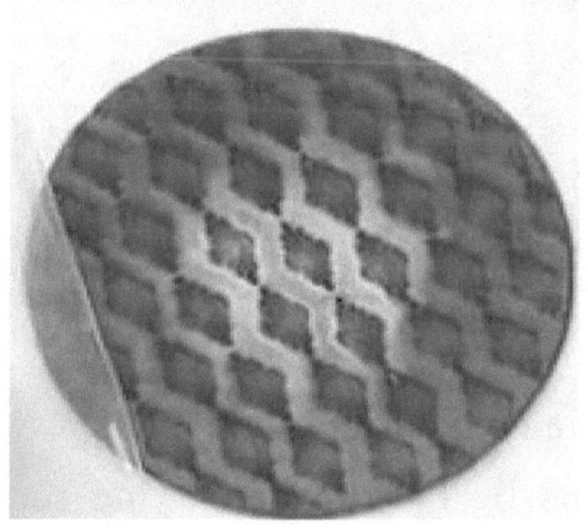

Let It Dry: Lay the color-blocked leather piece flat and allow it to dry completely. Avoid folding or manipulating the leather while drying to maintain the color blocks' clean edges.

Step 12: Finish and Protect (Optional): Apply a leather finish or conditioner to protect and enhance the colors once the leather is dry. Follow the instructions on the leather finish product for proper application.

Color blocking provides endless opportunities for creative expression, allowing you to play with various color combinations and geometric shapes to make a strong visual statement in your leather projects.

✓ ***Tie-Dyeing***

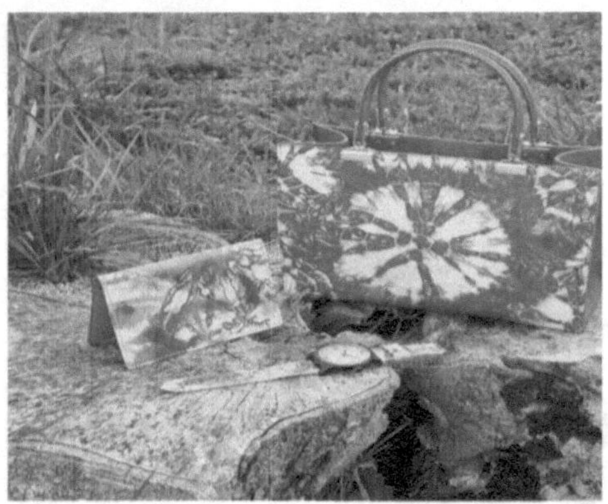

Tie-dyeing is a fun and experimental technique that allows you to create abstract patterns by twisting and tying the leather before applying the dye. This playful technique works well on small leather accessories, bracelets, and keychains, adding a touch of artistic flair to your designs.

To Achieve The Tie-Dye Effect:

Step 1:

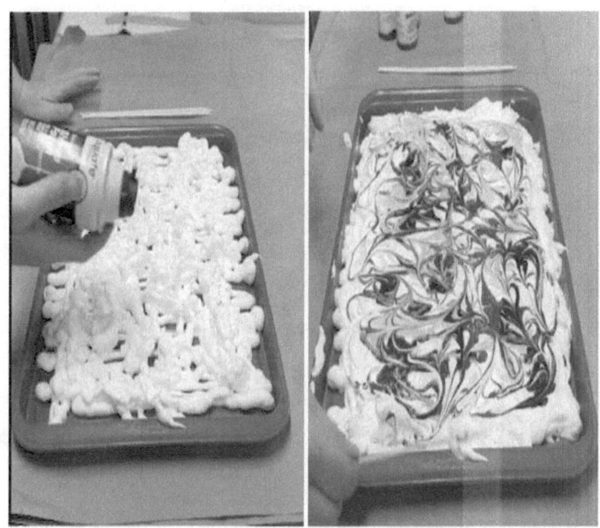

Prepare the dye: Prepare your dye solution according to the manufacturer's instructions. You can use different dye colors in separate containers to create various patterns.

Step 2: Lay out the leather: Lay the leather flat on a work surface. Ensure you have a protective covering under the leather to catch any excess dye that may drip through.

Step 3: Create patterns: Fold, scrunch, or twist the leather into the desired patterns. You can experiment with different folding techniques to achieve various effects.

Common Folding Techniques In Leatherworking

✓ *Accordion Fold*

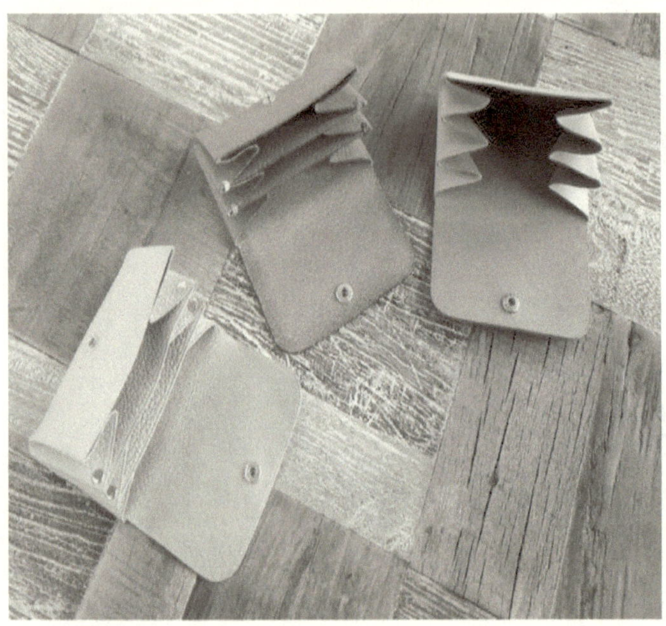

Fold the leather back and forth in a zigzag pattern to create an accordion fold. Hold the leather flat on your work surface, fold it forward, then backward, and continue alternating until you reach the desired length. This technique creates a series of parallel folds that can add texture and interest to your leather project.

✓ *Pleating*

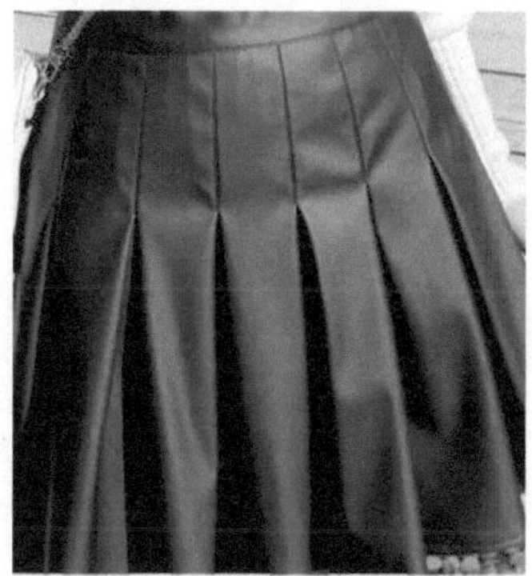

To achieve a pleated effect, make small, even folds along the length or width of the leather. You can create straight pleats by folding the leather in one direction or create chevron-style pleats by folding the leather in a V-shape. Pleating works well for adding dimension and structure to your leather pieces.

✓ *Triangular Folds*

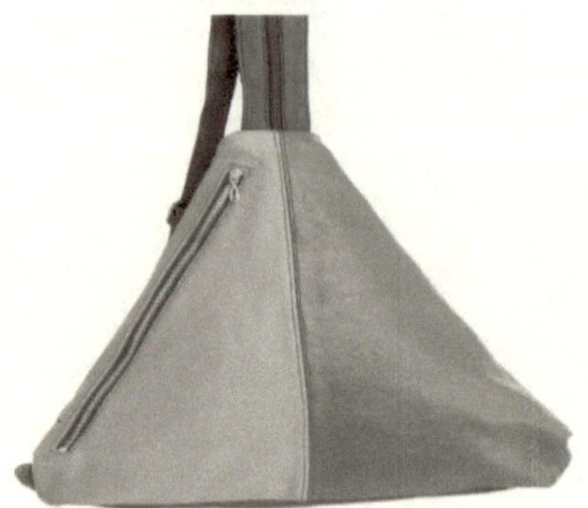

To make triangular folds, fold the leather at specific angles to create triangular shapes. For example, you can fold one leather corner diagonally to the opposite edge, forming a right triangle. This technique can create unique geometrical patterns on your leather surface.

✓ *Crumpling*

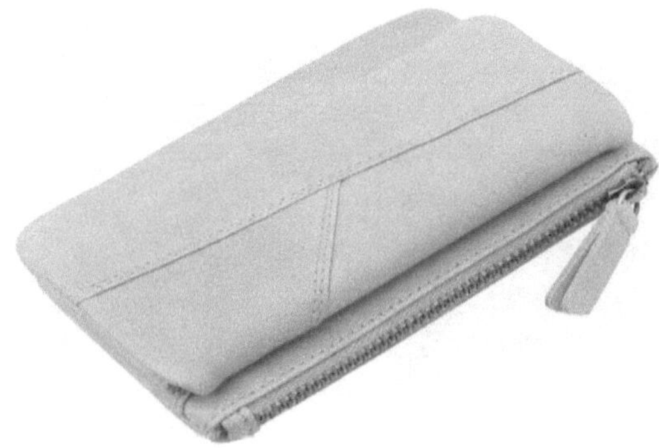

For a more organic and textured pattern, gently crumple the leather in your hands. Avoid pressing too hard to prevent creases. This technique works best with softer and more pliable leathers. Crumplings can add a weathered and distressed appearance to your leather projects.

✓ ***Roll Fold***

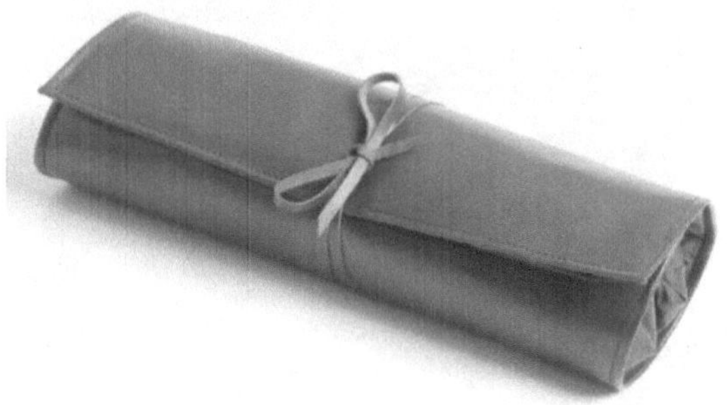

To create a roll fold, roll the leather into a cylindrical shape, similar to rolling up a piece of paper. This technique adds dimension and can create tube-like structures or decorative elements in leather pieces.

✓ *Diagonal Fold*

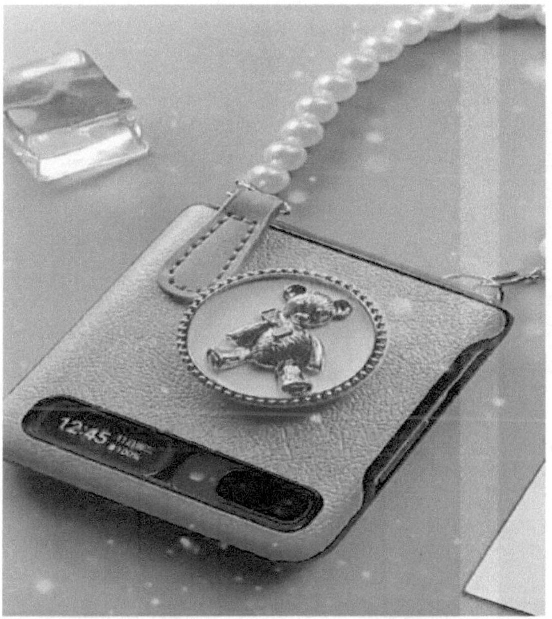

Fold the leather diagonally to create a diagonal pattern. Start by folding one corner of the leather to the opposite edge, forming a triangle. This technique can be used to create dynamic and angular designs.

✓ *Layered Folding*

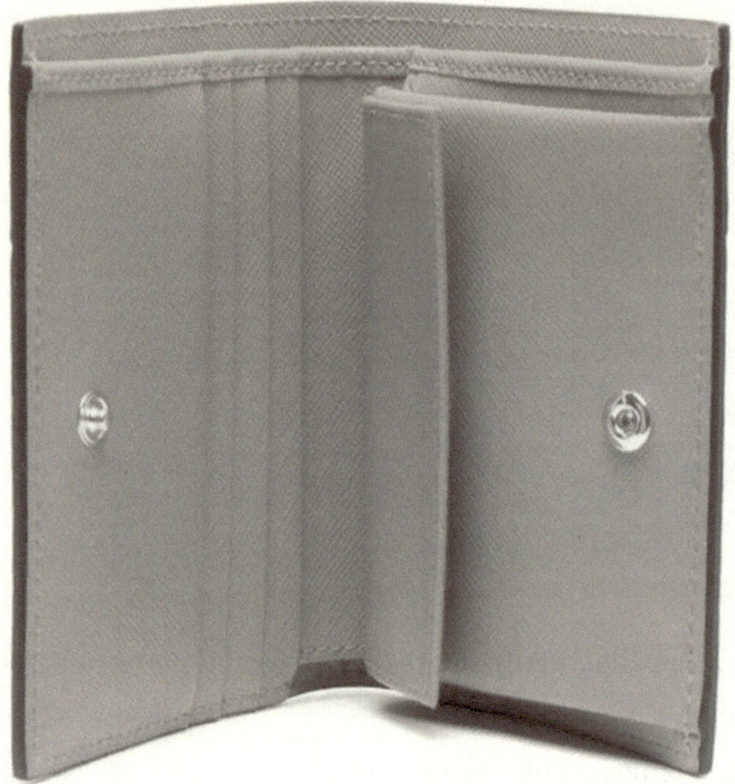

Stack multiple layers of leather and fold them together. This technique can add depth and dimension to your designs, especially when using leather of different colors or textures.

✓ ***Origami-inspired Folds***

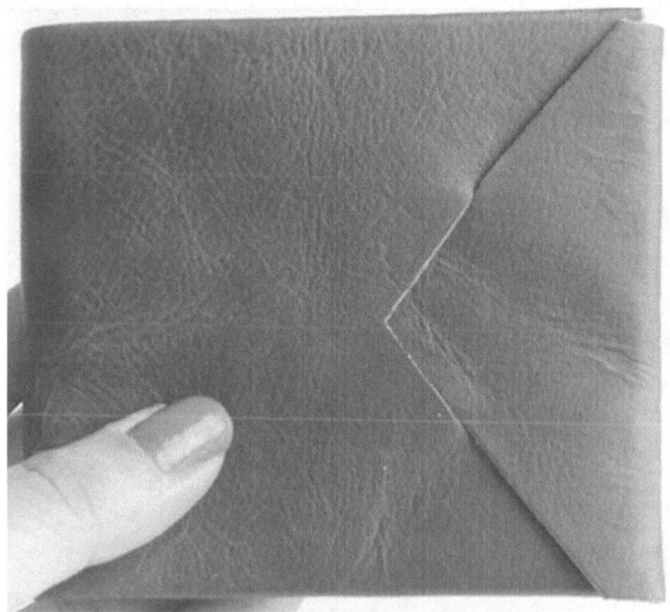

Take inspiration from origami techniques and fold the leather into intricate shapes and designs. Explore different origami folds like the petal, waterbomb, or bird base to create visually captivating patterns.

Step 4: Place on top of the dye: Carefully place the folded leather on top of the dye containers, ensuring that the areas you want to be dyed are in contact with the dye.

Step 5: Let it absorb the dye: Allow the leather to sit on top of the dye for a few minutes per the manufacturer's instructions. The dye will be absorbed into the exposed leather areas, creating the tie-dye effect.

Step 6: Check the colors: Lift the leather slightly to see if the colors develop as desired. Let it sit on the dye longer if you want more intense colors.

Step 7:

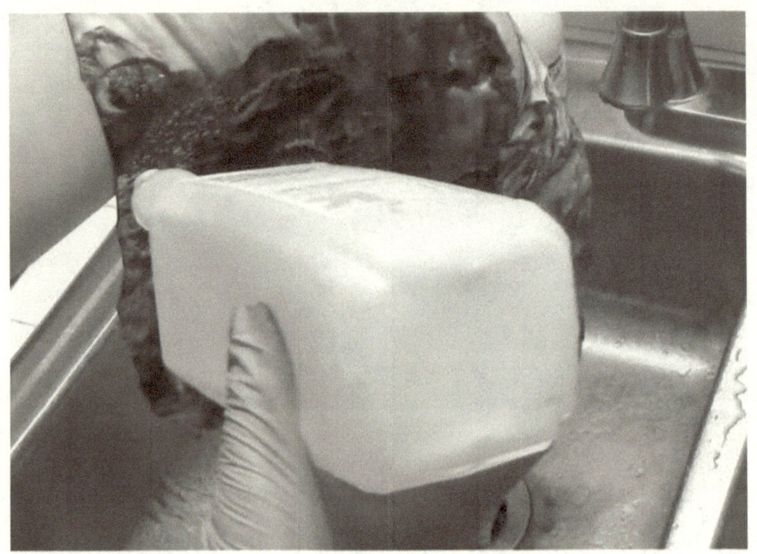

Rinse the leather: After achieving the desired colors, carefully lift and rinse it under running water to remove excess dye. You can also gently squeeze the leather to remove any remaining dye.

Step 8: Let it dry: Allow the leather to air dry completely before using or finishing it. Avoid wringing or twisting the leather, which may distort the tie-dye pattern.

Step 9: Apply finishes (optional): Depending on your project, you may apply a leather finish or sealant to protect the tie-dye design and give the leather a polished look.

By mastering these diverse leather dyeing techniques, you can elevate your leatherworking skills and create exceptional pieces that showcase your creativity and artistry. Enjoy the journey of exploring and experimenting with different dyeing techniques to make your leather projects stand out as works of art. The more you practice and refine your dyeing skills, the more confidence and proficiency you will gain in bringing your creative visions to life on leather.

Finishing

Finishing in leatherworking refers to applying various treatments and coatings to the surface of the leather to enhance its appearance, durability, and protection. Leather finishing helps achieve specific outcomes and ensures the final product is aesthetically pleasing and functional.

- **Common Leather Finishing Techniques And When They Are Used**

✓ ***Sealing and Protecting***: Leather is often sealed and protected with coatings like leather finishes, waxes, or acrylic sealants. These treatments create a protective barrier on the leather surface, guarding it against water, stains, and general wear and tear. Sealing is commonly used in leather goods such as bags, wallets, and belts to increase longevity and maintain a pristine appearance.

- ✓ ***Polishing***: Polishing leather enhances its shine and smoothness, giving it a refined and elegant finish. Various polishing compounds and creams can be applied to the leather surface, then buffed with a soft cloth or brush. Polishing is frequently employed in high-quality leather goods, shoes, and luxury leather accessories to achieve a luxurious and lustrous look.

- ✓ ***Edge*** Finishing: Edge finishing is done on the raw edges of leather pieces to create a neat and refined appearance. Burnishing, beveling, or edge paints smooth and seals the edges. This is especially important in projects like leather belts, where the edges are visible and must be aesthetically pleasing and durable.

- ✓ ***Antiquing***: Antiquing is a finishing technique used to create an aged or vintage appearance on leather. Special dyes or stains are applied to the leather, highlighting creases, folds, and contours, giving the leather a weathered or distressed look. Antiquing is often used in leather crafting projects that aim to achieve a rustic or old-world charm.

✓ ***Dyeing***: As mentioned earlier, dyeing is a crucial part of finishing, as it adds color and character to the leather. Leather dyeing can be done in various colors and shades to match the desired aesthetic of the final product.

✓ ***Burnishing***: This technique involves rubbing the leather edges with a burnishing tool or slicker to create a smooth and polished finish. This technique is often used on leather belts, wallets, and other items with visible edges.

✓ ***Embossing***: Embossing is a finishing technique where a pattern or design is pressed into the leather surface, creating a textured effect. This is commonly used in leather goods to add decorative elements and make them visually appealing.

Leather finishing techniques are utilized in various leatherworking projects, such as crafting accessories, garments, footwear, and home decor items. Each finishing method is chosen based on the specific requirements of the project and the desired outcome. Proper finishing not only enhances the appearance of the leather but also ensures its durability and longevity.

- **Overcoming Challenges in Leather Finishing**

As a beginner in leatherworking, you may encounter several challenges when finishing leather projects.

Here are some common challenges and strategies to overcome them:

- ✓ ***Uneven Finish***: Achieving an even finish can be difficult, especially if you're new to leatherworking. Uneven application of dyes, polishes, or sealants can produce blotchy or streaky finishes.

  Overcome: Practice on scrap pieces of leather to get a feel for applying the finish evenly. Use light and even strokes when applying dyes or polishes. Take your time and work in small sections to ensure consistent coverage. If you notice uneven spots, reapply the finish to achieve a smooth and uniform look.

- ✓ ***Overuse of Finish***: Applying too much finish can lead to a sticky or tacky surface, which is unpleasant and attracts dirt and grime.

  Overcome: Use a light hand when applying finishes. Remember that a little goes a long way, especially with dyes and polishes. If you accidentally apply too much finish, gently blot the excess with a clean cloth or sponge to remove any buildup.

- ✓ ***Edge Finishing Challenges***: Achieving smooth and polished edges can be challenging for beginners, and raw edges may look rough and unprofessional.

Overcome: Practice edge finishing techniques like burnishing or edge painting on scrap leather pieces. Invest in quality edge finishing tools like edge finishers (or edge slickers) and edge groovers, and use them carefully to create neat and refined edges. Take your time and be patient with this step, as well-finished edges can significantly enhance the overall appearance of your leather project.

✓ ***Color Matching***: Getting the exact color you want can be tricky, especially when dyeing leather. Different types of leather and their absorbent qualities can affect the final color.

Overcome: Perform color tests on scrap pieces of the same leather to see how the dye behaves and how the color turns out. Mix different dye shades if necessary to achieve the desired color. Remember that leather may appear slightly darker when wet, so allow the dyed leather to dry thoroughly before assessing the color.

✓ ***Stain or Dye Bleeding***: Some dyes or stains may bleed or transfer to other parts of the leather or surrounding materials.

Overcome: When using dyes or stains, be cautious about the potential for bleeding. Allow the dyed leather to dry completely before handling or using it in a project. If you're concerned about bleeding, apply a clear finish or sealer over the dyed surface to prevent color transfer.

- ✓ ***Limited Tools and Materials***: As a beginner, you may have limited tools and materials, making specific finishing techniques more challenging.

  Overcome: Start with basic finishing tools and materials and gradually expand your collection as you gain experience and tackle more complex projects. You can also explore alternative techniques or improvised tools to create yourself. For example, you can use household items like butter knives, spoon handles, or even a wooden dowel as burnishers to achieve a polished edge finish.

- ✓ ***Finishing Complex Shapes***: Achieving a consistent finish can be difficult when working on projects with intricate designs or complex shapes.

  Overcome: Take your time and work patiently on each project section. Use smaller brushes or applicators to reach tight corners and intricate details. Don't rush the finishing process; focus on maintaining a steady hand to ensure a professional-looking finish.

Remember that practice and patience are essential in leatherworking. As you encounter challenges, view them as opportunities to learn and improve your skills. You'll overcome these challenges and produce beautifully finished leather projects by being persistent and experimenting with different techniques.

Finishing Process

Step 1: Ensure Dyed Leather is Dry

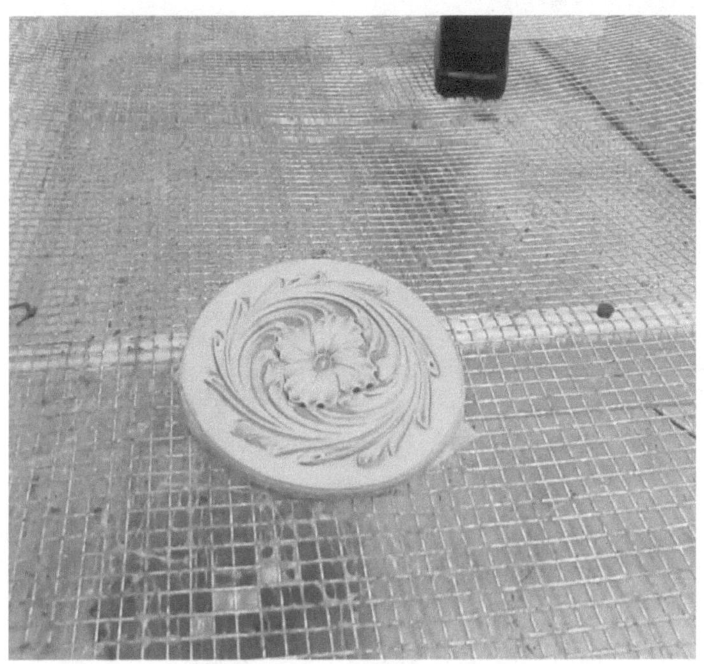

Before starting the finishing process, it's crucial to ensure that any leather dye you previously applied is completely dry. This step is essential because applying a damp leather finish can result in uneven absorption and potential color changes. To check if the leather is dry, lightly touch the dyed surface; it should feel dry to the touch without any transfer of color to your fingers.

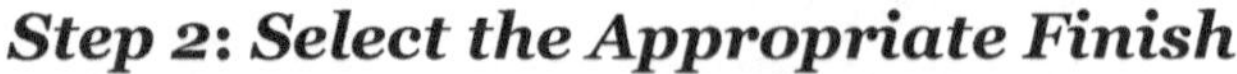

Step 2: Select the Appropriate Finish

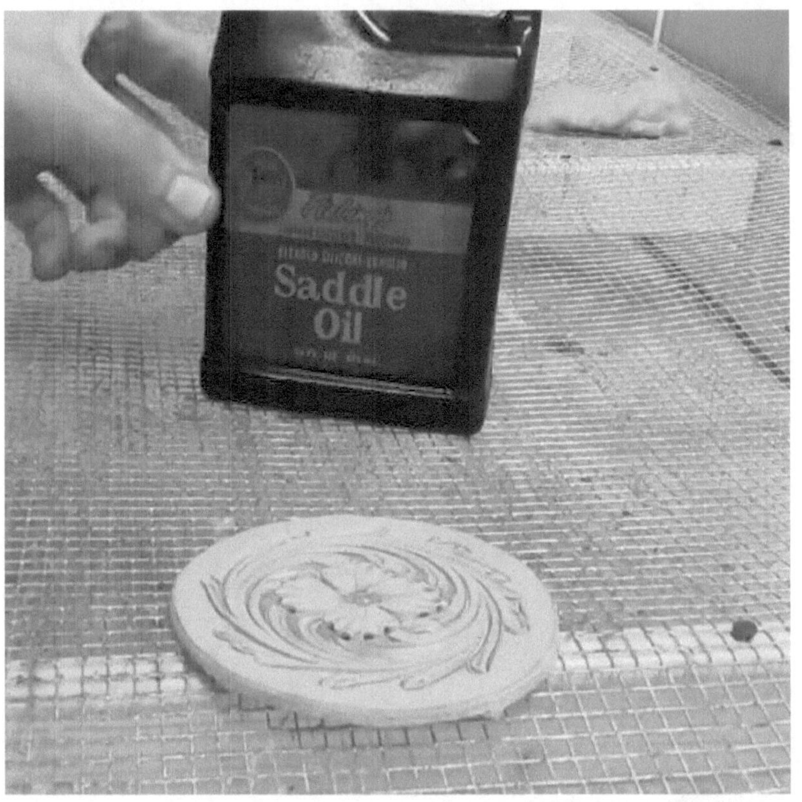

Choosing the right finish is vital for achieving your desired outcome. Consider the type of leather you're working with, the level of shine or protection you want, and the intended use of the finished leather item. Please read the labels or instructions on the finished product to understand its properties and suitability for your project. If you're unsure, start with a simple acrylic finish, which is versatile and beginner-friendly.

Step 3: Apply the Finish

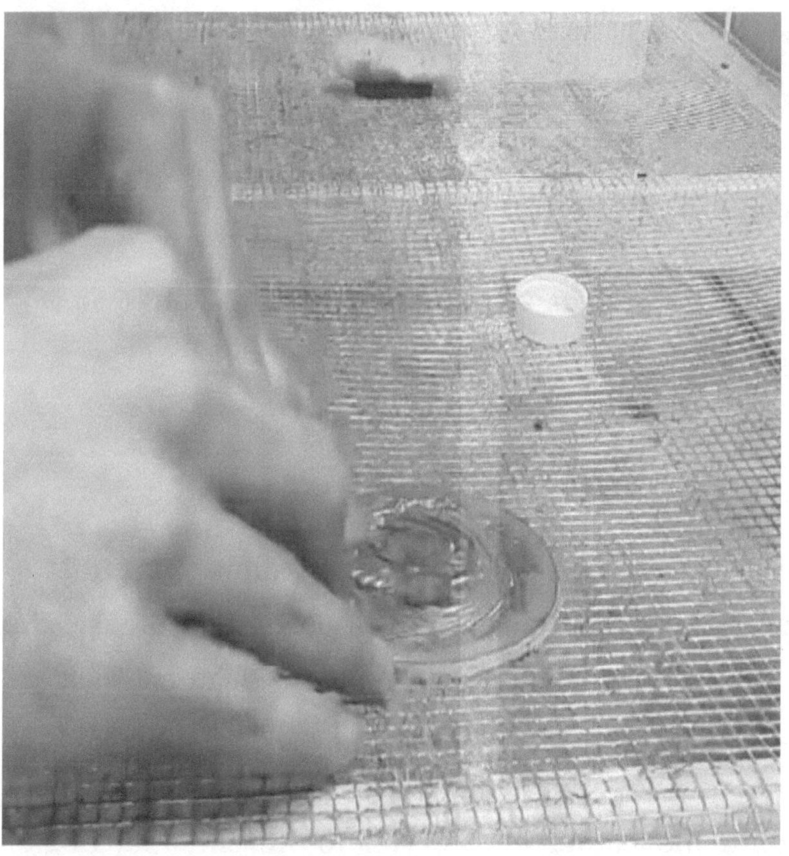

Dip your chosen applicator (such as a sponge, wool dauber, or brush) into the finish solution to apply the finish. Start applying the finish to the leather in even strokes, working in small sections. Avoid oversaturating the leather with the finish, leading to an uneven or sticky surface. Use light and gentle strokes for a more even application, gradually building up the finish as needed.

Step 4*: *Allow the Finish to Dry

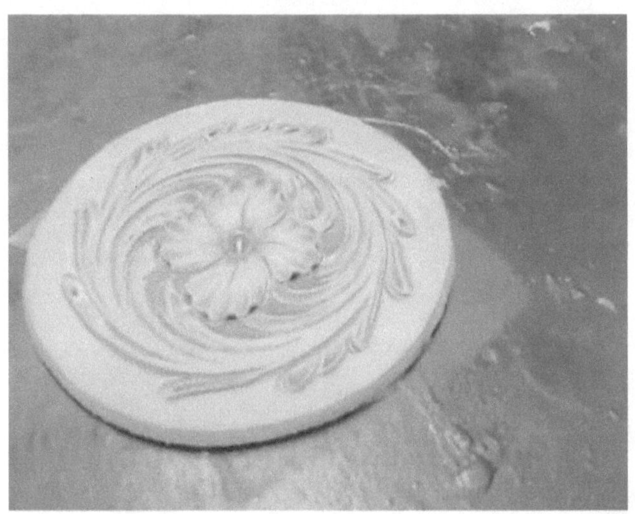

After applying the finish, be patient and allow the leather to dry completely. The drying time will depend on the specific finish you've used and environmental factors such as humidity and temperature. Follow the manufacturer's guidelines for the recommended drying time. Avoid touching or handling the leather while drying to prevent smudging or disrupting the finish.

Step 5: Buff the Leather

Once the finish has dried, you can enhance the shine and smoothness of the leather by buffing it. Take a soft cloth or rag and gently buff the leather in circular motions. Buffing helps to distribute the finish evenly and gives the leather a more polished appearance. If you prefer a matte finish, you can skip this step.

Step 6: Optional Additional Coats (Optional)

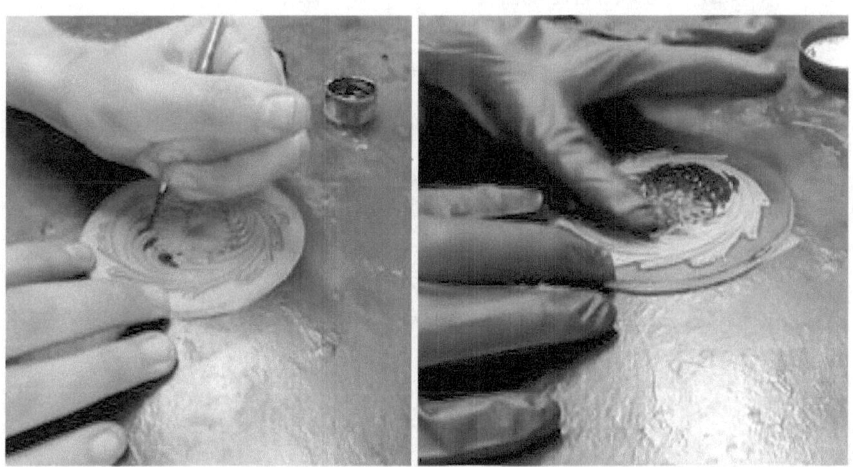

Depending on the type of finish you're using and the level of protection or sheen you desire, you may apply additional coats of the finish. If applying multiple coats, ensure each layer is fully dry before adding the next one. Additional coats can increase the durability and longevity of the finish, especially for items that will experience frequent use or exposure to the elements.

Step 7: Allow the Finish to Cure (Optional)

Specific finishes may require curing to achieve their complete protective properties. If the manufacturer's instructions specify a curing time, follow them. Curing bonds the finish with the leather, enhancing its resistance to water, stains, and wear. Be patient and avoid using or handling the finished leather until the curing process is complete.

Step 8: Enjoy Your Finished Leather

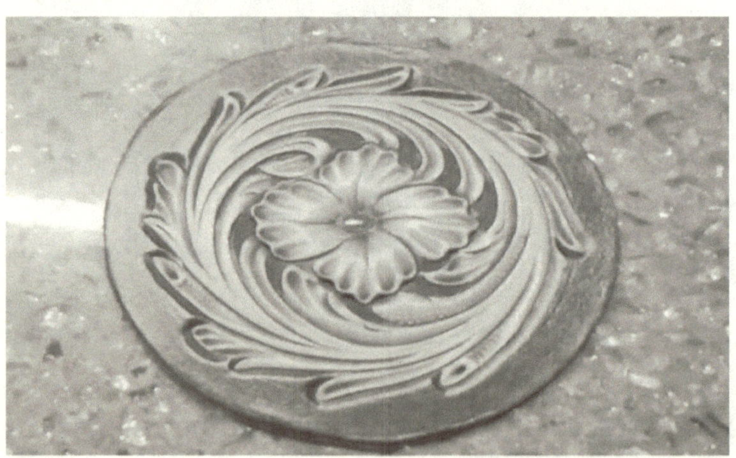

Congratulations! Your leather project is now beautifully finished and ready for use. Take pride in your creation and enjoy the satisfaction of turning raw leather into a functional and aesthetically pleasing piece.

You have the knowledge and skills to create remarkable leather pieces by mastering these essential leatherworking techniques. Practice each technique diligently, allowing your creativity to flourish as you incorporate them into your unique designs. Remember, mastery comes with time and experience, so embrace the journey and enjoy transforming leather into works of art.

Chapter 8: Care and Maintenance of Leather

This section will delve into preserving and protecting your valuable leather goods. Leather is a unique and timeless material that requires proper care to maintain its natural beauty and extend its lifespan.

This chapter will explore various essential techniques and step-by-step guides to help you care for your leather items. Whether you own leather shoes, bags, jackets, furniture, or accessories, these techniques will empower you to keep your leather goods pristine and stylish for years.

Understanding the importance of caring for leather, we will cover routine cleaning, conditioning, and protection methods. Additionally, we will address specific challenges, such as handling stains and moisture issues and preventing long-term damage.

This chapter will equip you with the knowledge and skills to nurture and preserve your cherished leather possessions. Embrace the leather care and maintenance journey, and discover the joy of owning timeless pieces that age gracefully and exude enduring elegance. Let's begin our exploration into the art of leather care together.

Importance of Leather Care

Caring for your leather items is crucial for several reasons. Let's delve into why proper care is essential for the longevity and aesthetic appeal of your leather creations.

- **Prolonging Lifespan**

Proper care and maintenance are essential for prolonging the lifespan of your leather items. Leather is a durable material, but without regular care, it can succumb to wear and tear, significantly reducing its longevity. By implementing appropriate care practices like regular cleaning, you can protect the leather from common issues like drying, cracking, and fading, ensuring that your creations stand the test of time and remain in excellent condition for years.

- **Enhancing Durability**

Well-maintained leather is more resistant to daily wear and tear. Conditioning the leather replenish essential oils that keep it supple and flexible. This increased flexibility reduces the likelihood of cracks and tear, making your leather items more durable and resilient to rough handling. Whether it's a leather bag, wallet, or belt, regular care enhances the overall durability, ensuring they can withstand regular use and retain their shape.

- **RetainingAesthetic Appeal**

Leather's natural beauty lines in its rich texture, color variations, and luxurious feel. Regular care helps retain the leather's aesthetic appeal and keep it looking its best. When you clean and condition leather, you prevent dirt buildup, stains, and discoloration, which ensures that your items maintain their original allure. By preserving the leather's luster and suppleness, you can enjoy the beauty of your creations and showcase them with pride.

- **Protecting Against Environmental Damage**

Leather is susceptible to damage from environmental factors such as sunlight, heat, and moisture. UV rays can fade and weaken the leather's surface, while excess moisture can lead to mold and mildew growth and proper care involves protecting your leather items from these elements. Using leather protectants with UV inhibitors shields the leather from harmful sun rays, and conditioning products act as a barrier against moisture, preventing damage caused by humidity.

- **Personal Investment**

Leatherworking is an art form that requires creativity, skill, and dedication. The items you create are a reflection of your craftsmanship and hold sentimental value. Proper care is an investment in your artistry, as it preserves your hard work and dedication. By ensuring your leather pieces remain in excellent condition, you can showcase your skills and craftsmanship to others while taking pride in the timeless beauty of your creations.

- **Health and Hygiene**

Proper care and maintenance of leather items are essential to ensure a healthier and more hygienic environment, especially if you have allergies or sensitivities. Neglected leather items can collect dust, dirt, and allergens, posing potential health risks. Regular cleaning and maintenance help eliminate these particles, keeping the surroundings cleaner and safer.

Moreover, mold and mildew growth on leather can trigger respiratory issues and allergies. It's crucial to isolate the affected leather items from other belongings to prevent the further spread of mold spores. Taking prompt action and employing appropriate cleaning methods like regular dusting and brushing can salvage the leather and maintain its safety and pleasantness.

- **Cost-Effectiveness**

Investing in high-quality leather is often more expensive, but taking proper care, such as conditioning, can make it a cost-effective choice in the long run. Well-maintained leather lasts significantly longer, reducing the need for frequent replacements. By protecting your leather items from premature wear and damage, you can save money in the long term and enjoy the longevity of your cherished leather pieces.

Techniques for Leather Care and Maintenance

Here we will delve into a comprehensive range of techniques to help you care for your leather items effectively. Whether you own leather shoes, bags, jackets, or furniture, understanding how to clean, condition, and protect your leather will ensure they remain in excellent condition and stand the test of time.

Here are ways of caring for and maintaining your leather:

- **Cleaning Leather**

Cleaning leather is an essential part of proper leather care and maintenance. Regular cleaning helps remove dirt, dust, and surface stains, keeping the leather in good condition and preserving its appearance and longevity. Proper cleaning ensures your leather items remain clean, vibrant, and ready for use for years.

Now, let's proceed with the cleaning process for leather.

✓ ***Step 1:***

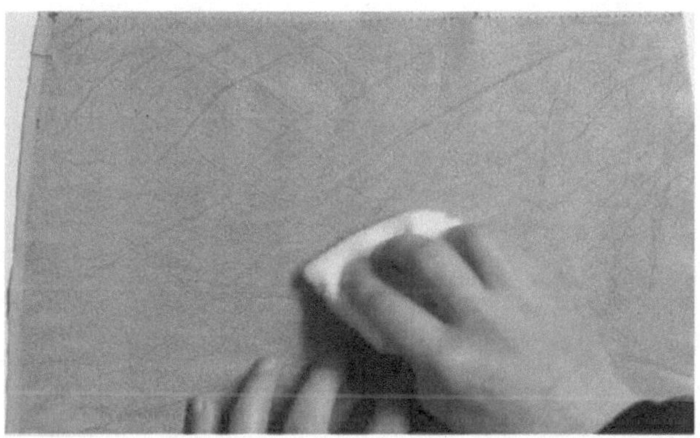

Gently dust off the leather surface with a soft, dry cloth or a soft brush to remove loose dirt and dust particles. Dust can act as an abrasive material, so this initial step prevents potential scratching during the cleaning process.

✓ ***Step 2:***

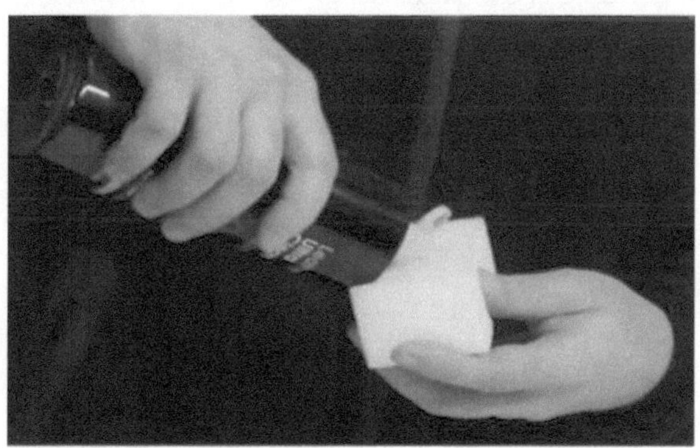

Dampen a clean, soft cloth with the diluted cleaner, ensuring it's not soaking wet. Excess water can cause damage to leather, so ***a damp but not wet cloth*** is ideal. Avoid using too much pressure while applying the cleaner to prevent soaking the leather.

✓ ***Step 3***:

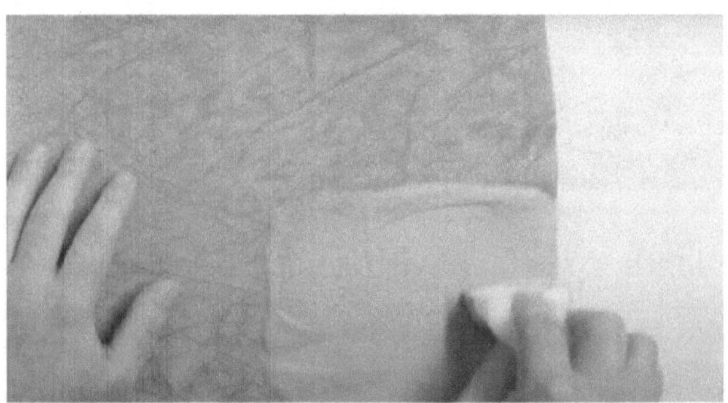

With the damp cloth, wipe the leather surface, working in gentle circular motions. Avoid excessive scrubbing or rubbing, as this can damage the leather's delicate surface. Pay extra attention to areas with visible stains or spills.

✓ ***Step 4:***

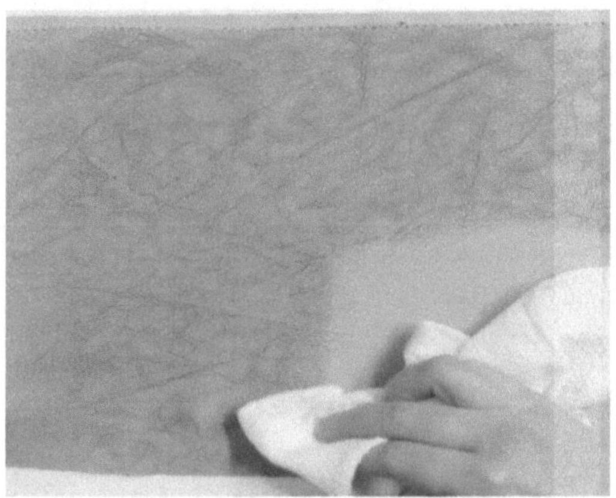

Use a separate clean, damp cloth to wipe off any residual cleaner from the leather. Thoroughly removing the cleaning solution prevents unwanted residues from affecting the leather's texture and finish.

✓ ***Step 5:***

Allow the leather to air dry naturally, away from direct sunlight or heat sources. Heat and sunlight can cause the leather to dry out and lose its natural oils, leading to cracks and fading. ***Patience is key in this step*** to ensure the leather dries evenly and safely.

For deeper cleaning, prepare a mild leather cleaner suitable for your leather type. Follow the product instructions to ensure compatibility and effectiveness. Different leather types, such as full-grain and top-grain, may require a pH-balanced leather cleaner or a mild soap and water solution. Avoid harsh chemicals that can strip away natural oils and damage the leather. ***Always do a spot test*** in an inconspicuous area before applying the cleaner to the entire surface.

Let's now explore another technique:

- **Conditioning Leather**

Conditioning leather is a crucial step in leather care that involves applying a specialized conditioner ***to keep the leather soft, supple, and moisturized***. Leather is a natural material that contains oils, and over time, these oils can dry out and cause the leather to become stiff and susceptible to cracking. Conditioning replenishes these natural oils, restoring the leather's flexibility and preventing drying.

Here is a conditioning process:

✓ ***Step 1:***

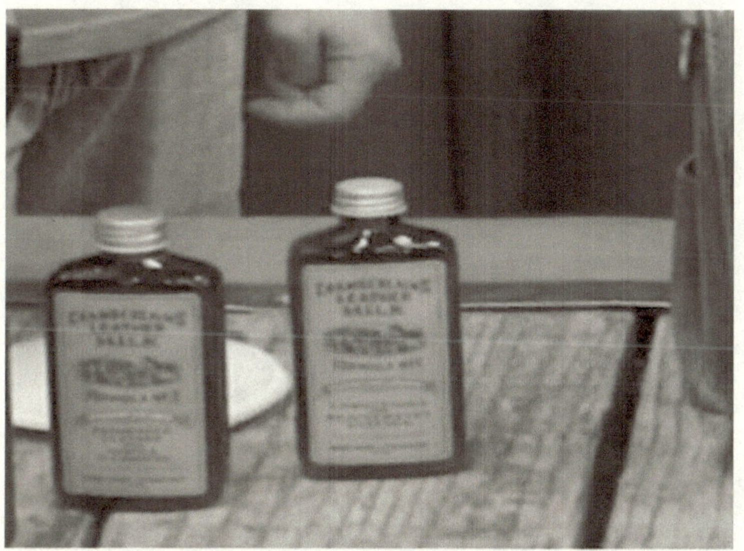

Choose a high-quality leather conditioner suitable for your leather type. Look for products that contain natural oils and waxes to replenish the leather's moisture and flexibility. Conditioning is essential to prevent the leather from drying out and being stiff or brittle over time.

✓ ***Step 2:***

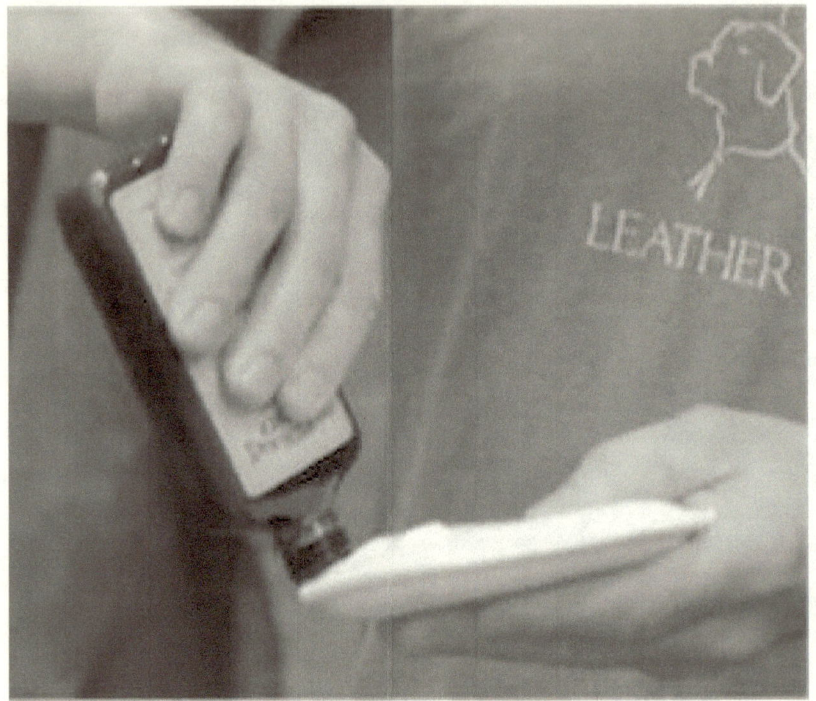

Apply a small amount of conditioner to a soft, clean cloth or sponge: this prevents over-saturation and ensures even application across the leather surface. Always start with a small amount and add more if needed.

✓ ***Step 3:***

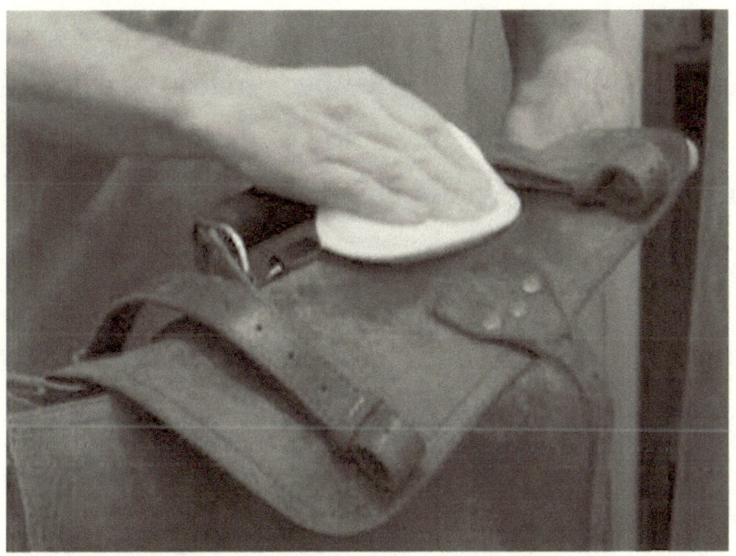

Rub the conditioner into the leather surface using gentle circular motions. Concentrate on areas that may be prone to dryness or cracking, such as seams and creases. The circular motions help the leather absorb the conditioner evenly and effectively.

✓ ***Step 4:***

Allow the conditioner to be absorbed by the leather for the recommended time mentioned in the product instructions. This duration allows the conditioner to penetrate the leather's fibers, nourishing it from within and restoring its suppleness.

✓ ***Step 5:***

Wipe off any excess conditioner with a clean, dry cloth. Leaving excess conditioner on the leather can lead to a sticky or greasy surface, so thorough wiping is essential. Ensure there are no visible residues left behind.

✓ ***Step 6:***

Let the leather sit for few hours to allow the conditioner to penetrate and nourish the material fully. This resting period ensures that the leather absorbs the conditioner completely, leaving it soft, supple, and well-nourished.

Guide to Cleaning and Conditioning Different Types of Leather

- **Cleaning and Conditioning Top-Grain and Full-Grain Leather**

✓ ***Cleaning:***

1. Start by dusting off the leather's surface with a dry soft material or a soft brush. Doing this removes any loose dirt, dust, or debris that could scratch the leather during cleaning.

2. Add mild soap to water for minor stains or spills to create a soapy solution. Use a sponge or soft cloth to dampen it

with the solution, wringing out any excess water. Blot the stained sections, beginning on the outer ends and working to the center. Avoid massaging vigorously to avoid damaging the leather's finish or texture.

3. Use another clean, damp cloth to wipe away the soapy residue from the leather. Remove all traces of soap, as it can dry out the leather if left on the surface.

4. Pat dry the cleaned area with a clean cloth, removing excess moisture. Allow the leather to air dry naturally in a cool, well-ventilated area. Avoid using direct heat sources or sunlight to speed up the drying process, as they can make the leather dry out and cause cracks.

✓ ***Conditioning:***

1. Once the leather is dry, apply a conditioner designed explicitly for top-grain and full-grain leather. Conditioning helps replenish the natural oils in the leather, keeping it soft, supple, and moisturized.

2. Pour some conditioner onto an applicator pad or a soft, lint-free fabric. Using circular motions, smoothly rub it into the leather, paying more attention to one small section at a go. Ensure even coverage and avoid applying too much conditioner, as excess product may not be absorbed and can leave a greasy residue.

3. Let the conditioner be absorbed by the leather, following the manufacturer's recommended time (usually a few minutes). This step allows the leather to soak in the beneficial properties of the conditioner.

4. After the recommended time, buff the leather gently with a dry clean cloth to enhance its shine. Buffing also helps remove any excess conditioner, leaving the leather with a smooth and polished appearance.

- **Cleaning and Conditioning Bonded Leather**

✓ ***Cleaning:***

1. Begin by dusting off the bonded leather's surface with a dry soft cloth or brush. Doing this removes loose dirt and debris without causing any damage to the bonded leather's polyurethane coating.

2. Add mild soap to water for minor stains or spills to create a soapy solution. Dampen a soft cloth with the solution and gently blot the stained area, avoiding excessive rubbing.

3. Use another clean, damp cloth to remove the bonded leather's soapy residue. Ensure that no soap is left on the surface.

4. Pat dry the cleaned area with a clean cloth, ensuring no excess moisture remains on the bonded leather's surface.

✓ ***Conditioning:***

1. Unlike genuine leather, bonded leather typically has a polyurethane coating layer; therefore, ***it does not require conditioning***. The polyurethane acts as a protective barrier, and applying leather conditioner may not be absorbed by the bonded leather, leading to a sticky or greasy surface. Avoid using leather conditioner on bonded leather.

- **Cleaning and Conditioning Genuine Leather**

✓ ***Cleaning:***

1. Start by dusting off the genuine leather's surface with a dry soft cloth or brush. This step removes loose debris, dust, or dirt from the leather.

2. Add mild soap to water for minor stains or spills to create a soapy solution. Dampen a soft fabric with the solution and gently blot the stained area, avoiding excessive rubbing.

3. Use another clean, damp cloth to wipe away the soapy residue from the leather. Ensure that no soap is left on the surface.

4. Pat dry the cleaned area with a clean cloth, ensuring no excess moisture remains on the genuine leather's surface.

✓ ***Conditioning:***

1. Once the leather is completely dry, apply a conditioner designed explicitly for genuine leather. Conditioning helps replenish the natural oils in the leather, keeping it soft, supple, and moisturized.

2. Pour some conditioner onto an applicator pad or a soft, lint-free fabric. In circular motions, smoothly rub it into the leather, paying more attention to one small section before moving to the next. Ensure even coverage and avoid applying too much conditioner, as excess product may not be absorbed and can leave a greasy residue.

3. Let the conditioner be absorbed by the leather, following the manufacturer's recommended time (usually a few minutes). Doing this allows the leather to soak in the beneficial properties of the conditioner.

4. After the recommended time, buff the leather gently with a dry clean cloth to enhance its shine. Buffing also helps to remove any excess conditioner, leaving the leather with a smooth and polished appearance.

5. Remember to test any cleaning or conditioning method on a small, inconspicuous leather area first to ensure it doesn't cause damage or discoloration. Proper cleaning and conditioning help maintain the beauty and longevity of leather items, making them look their best and last for years.

Let's dive into the third technique:

Protecting Leather from Environmental Factors

Leather is susceptible to damage from sunlight, moisture, and other environmental factors.

Let's explore how you can protect your leather items from these elements:

- **Protecting Leather from Moisture**

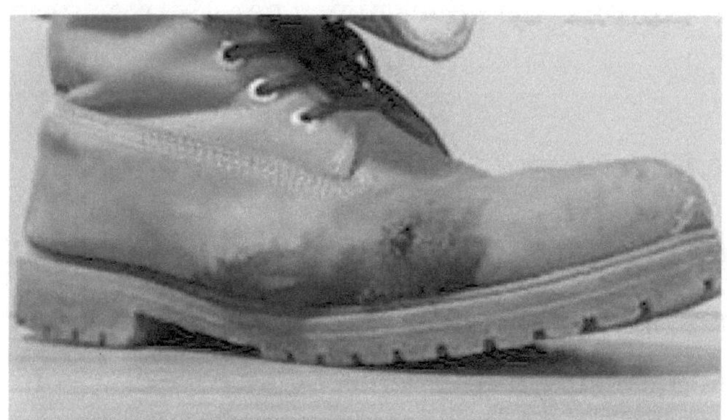

✓ ***Choose Proper Leather***

The type of leather used plays a significant role in its resistance to moisture. ***Full-grain and top-grain leather*** have a natural surface layer that provides some protection against water. These high-quality leathers are ideal for items that may come into contact with moisture. Avoid using suede or nubuck leather for such items, as they are more delicate and susceptible to water damage.

✓ ***Use a Leather Protector***

Leather protectors or ***waterproofing sprays*** create a protective barrier on the surface of the leather, making it more resistant to moisture and spills.

When using a leather protector, ensure the leather is clean and free from dust or debris to ensure proper adhesion. Follow the manufacturer's instructions on application and reapplication, as the protective effect may wear off over time and with regular use.

✓ ***Avoid Direct Exposure***

Keep leather items from direct exposure to water, rain, and high-humidity environments. If you know you'll be in a wet environment, consider using a different bag or covering your leather shoes with protective shoe covers. Avoid leaving leather items where they are likely to get wet, such as near open windows during rainstorms.

✓ ***Wipe Off Moisture Promptly***

When your leather item comes into contact with water or any other liquid, act quickly to minimize moisture absorption. Use a clean, dry cloth to gently blot the affected area, removing as much moisture as possible. Avoid rubbing the leather, as it can spread moisture and lead to more extensive damage.

✓ ***Air Dry Properly***

If your leather item gets wet, avoid using artificial heat sources like hairdryers, heaters, or direct sunlight to dry it. Heat can cause the leather to shrink, warp, or crack. Instead, let the item air dry at room temperature in a well-ventilated area. Placing the item on a towel or absorbent can help wick away excess moisture.

- **Dealing with Moisture Issues in Leather**

✓ ***Addressing Light Moisture Exposure:***

1) Blot the Leather: If your leather item gets slightly damp or has a small spill, immediately blot the affected area with a dry cloth. Blotting helps absorb the moisture, preventing it from seeping deeper into the leather.

2) Air Dry: After blotting, allow the leather to air dry naturally in a well-aerated space. Avoid using heat or fans to speed up the process, as they may make the leather dry too quickly and lead to damage.

3) Condition the Leather: Apply a suitable leather conditioner once the leather has dried completely. Conditioning restores the natural oils in the leather, maintaining its flexibility and preventing it from becoming stiff or prone to cracking.

✓ ***Handling Heavy Moisture Exposure:***

1) Blot and Absorb: If your leather item gets thoroughly wet or soaked, promptly blot off excess moisture with a dry cloth. Use a gentle pressing motion to remove as much water as possible.

2) Stuff the Item: For larger leather items, such as bags or shoes, stuff them with crumpled newspaper, paper towels, or absorbent materials. The stuffing helps draw out moisture from the inside of the item, preventing it from becoming waterlogged.

3) Air Dry Gradually: Allow the leather item to dry gradually in a well-ventilated area. Never use direct heat or place the item in direct sunlight, as it can cause the leather to shrink or crack.

4) Avoid Distortion: While the leather is still damp, gently reshape the item to its original form. Doing this helps prevent any permanent distortion caused by moisture.

5) Use a Leather Conditioner: Apply a conditioner after the leather has dried completely to restore its suppleness and maintain its integrity. After heavy moisture exposure, conditioning is essential to prevent the leather from drying out excessively.

✓ ***Mold and Mildew Prevention and Removal:***

1) Preventive Measures: Store leather pieces in a cool, dry place with good ventilation to prevent mold and mildew growth. Avoid keeping leather items in dark, damp, or poorly ventilated areas, as these conditions promote mold and mildew growth.

2) Cleaning Mold and Mildew: If you discover mold or mildew on your leather item, immediately remove it. Create a cleaning solution by mixing equal parts white vinegar and water. Use the mixture to dampen a soft fabric and gently wipe the affected area. After cleaning, allow the leather to dry thoroughly.

3) Use Anti-Fungal Solutions: If mold and mildew persist, it's best to consult a professional leather cleaner or

restorer. They may use specialized anti-fungal solutions that remove the growth without damaging the leather.

By following these detailed guidelines, you can effectively protect your leather items from moisture damage and handle moisture issues with care. Remember, prevention is vital to preserving the beauty and longevity of your leather goods.

- **Avoiding Extreme Temperatures**

Keep your leather items away from direct sunlight or prolonged exposure to UV rays. Sunlight can cause the leather's color to fade and lead to drying and cracking.

To protect your leather items from sunlight damage, follow these guidelines:

✓ Avoid Prolonged Sun Exposure: Limit your leather items' time in direct sunlight. Keep them away from windows, doors, or other areas with intense sunlight, if possible. This practice is essential for leather furniture, bags, and clothing.

✓ Create Shade: Suppose your leather objects are placed near windows or exposed to sunlight during certain times. Consider using curtains, blinds, or shades to create a barrier between the leather and direct sunlight.

✓ Use UV Protection Products: Specialized leather protectants and conditioners with UV protection properties are available. Applying these products can create a shield against UV rays, preserving the leather's color and preventing damage.

✓ Rotate Leather Items: If you have leather furniture or accessories in a room with ample sunlight, rotate their positions periodically. Doing this will ensure that all leather areas receive equal exposure to sunlight, preventing uneven fading.

✓ Store Leather in Shade: When storing leather items for an extended period, choose a shaded space away from direct UV rays. Optimal storage locations include closets, cabinets, or drawers not exposed to sunlight.

- **How to Deal with Sunlight Damage to Leather**

Despite your best efforts, sunlight damage may occur over time. If you notice fading, dryness, or cracking on your leather items, follow these steps to address the damage:

1) Clean the Leather: Clean the leather item using a gentle leather cleaner or mild soap and water solution before attempting any restoration. Removing dirt and dust will help you assess the extent of the damage.

2) Condition the Leather: Once the leather is clean and dry, apply a leather conditioner designed explicitly for restoring dry or sun-damaged leather. The conditioner will moisturize the leather, making it more supple and reducing the appearance of cracks.

3) Use Leather Rejuvenators: Consider using leather rejuvenators or restorers that contain color pigments to address fading. These products can help restore the leather's original color and improve its appearance.

4) Test on a Hidden Area: Before applying restoration products to the entire leather item, test them on a small, inconspicuous area to ensure compatibility and desired results.

Let's tackle the fourth technique:

Proper Storage and Handling Techniques

Here are the techniques to help you when it comes to storing and handling your leather items:

- **Technique 1:**

Store your leather items in a cool, dry place, away from direct sunlight and heat sources. Choose a location with consistent temperature and humidity levels to preserve the leather's quality. Avoid storing leather items in basements, attics, or garages, as these areas are prone to temperature fluctuations and moisture.

- **Technique 2:**

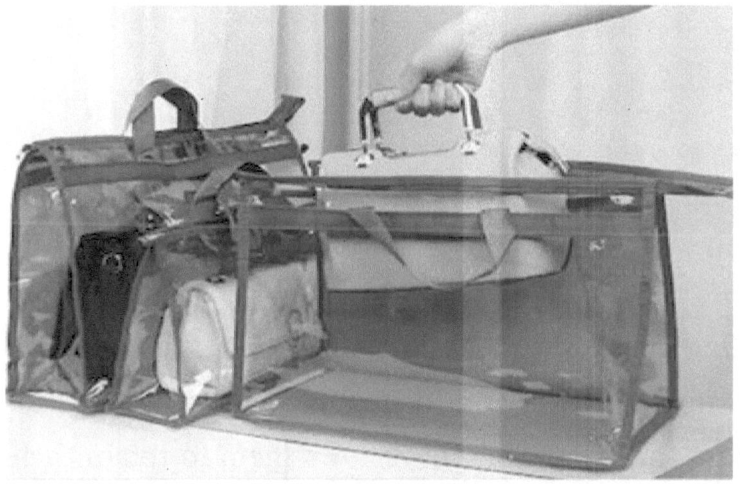

Use breathable storage bags or cloth covers to protect the leather from dust while allowing air circulation. Avoid plastic bags, as they can trap moisture and promote mold growth: Leather needs to breathe, and proper air circulation prevents musty odors and mold development.

- **Technique 3:**

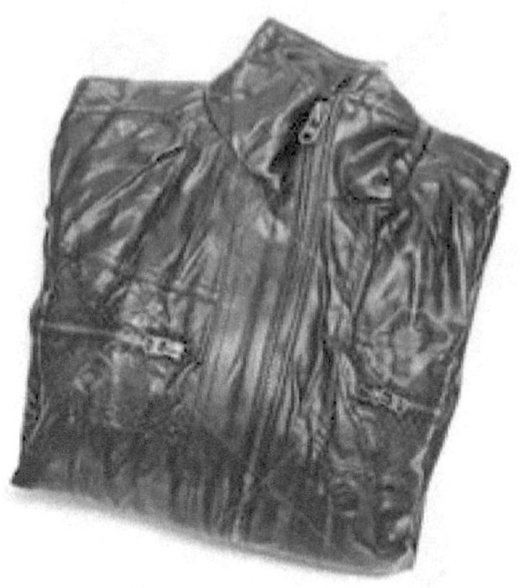

Avoid folding or compressing leather items excessively, as this can cause creases and distortions in the material. Instead, store them in a way that allows them to retain their original shape. Use supports or fillers, such as tissue paper or acid-free paper, to maintain the item's shape if needed.

We can now dive into the last technique:

Repair and Restoration

Repair and restoration of leather are essential aspects of leather care, especially for vintage or well-loved leather items that have developed wear and tear over time. Properly repairing and restoring leather can breathe new life into old

quality. Avoid storing leather items in basements, attics, or garages, as these areas are prone to temperature fluctuations and moisture.

- **Technique 2:**

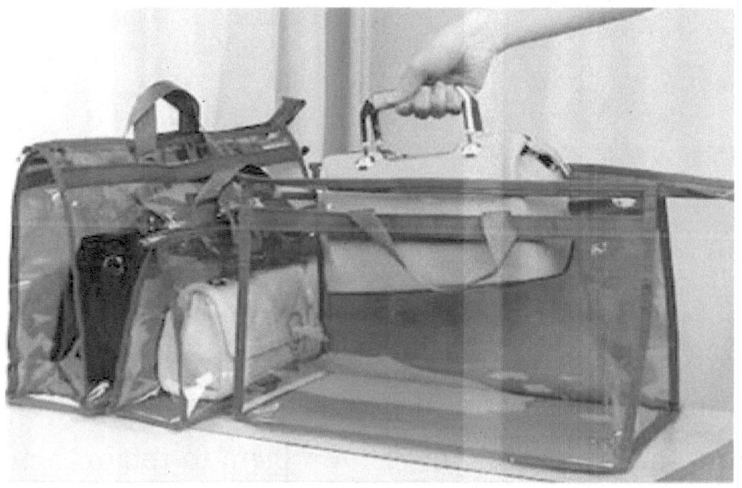

Use breathable storage bags or cloth covers to protect the leather from dust while allowing air circulation. Avoid plastic bags, as they can trap moisture and promote mold growth: Leather needs to breathe, and proper air circulation prevents musty odors and mold development.

- **Technique 3:**

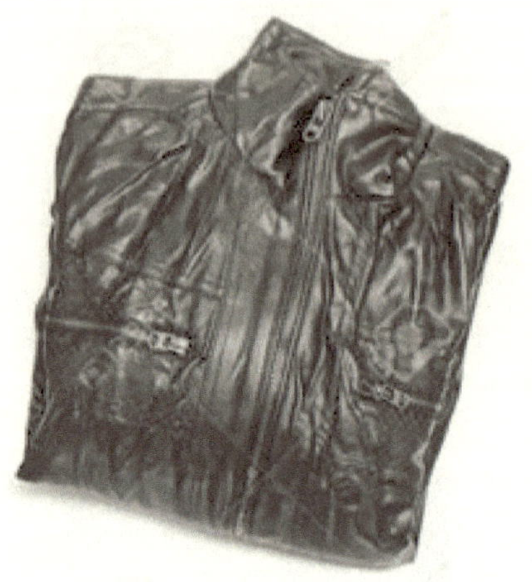

Avoid folding or compressing leather items excessively, as this can cause creases and distortions in the material. Instead, store them in a way that allows them to retain their original shape. Use supports or fillers, such as tissue paper or acid-free paper, to maintain the item's shape if needed.

We can now dive into the last technique:

Repair and Restoration

Repair and restoration of leather are essential aspects of leather care, especially for vintage or well-loved leather items that have developed wear and tear over time. Properly repairing and restoring leather can breathe new life into old pieces, extending their usability and preserving their unique character.

Here are repair and restoration techniques for leather:

- **Assessment of Damage**

Before starting any repair or restoration work, carefully assess the extent of damage to the leather item. Identify areas of concern, such as scratches, scuffs, tears, or color fading. Understanding the condition of the leather will help you determine the appropriate techniques needed for restoration.

- **Cleaning and Preparation**

Begin the restoration process by thoroughly cleaning the leather. Use a gentle leather cleaner or mild soap and water solution to remove dirt, grime, and surface stains. Ensure the leather is completely dry before proceeding with any repairs.

- **Color Restoration**

Consider color restoration techniques if the leather has faded or lost color. Leather dyes or colorants can bring back the original or a new desired color to the leather item. It is essential to match the color accurately and apply the dye evenly.

- **Repairing Scratches and Scuffs**

Minor scratches and scuffs can be addressed using leather repair kits with color-matched filler and sealant. Apply the filler to the affected areas and carefully blend it with the surrounding leather. Follow up with the sealant to protect the repaired spots.

- **Fixing Tears and Rips**

For small tears or rips, you can use leather glue or adhesive specifically designed for leather repair. Apply a thin layer of glue to the torn edges and press them until the glue sets. You may require a leather patch for larger tears, and it should be carefully stitched or glued into place.

- **Conditioning and Nourishing**

After the repairs, condition the entire leather item with a suitable leather conditioner. Conditioning helps moisturize the leather, restoring its suppleness and preventing future cracks or dryness.

- **Buffing and Polishing**

For a final touch, buff, and polish the restored leather item to enhance its shine and smoothness. Use a soft cloth or a horsehair brush to achieve a glossy finish.

Remember,

Successful leather repair and restoration require patience, precision, and suitable materials. You can continue enjoying their beauty and functionality by properly caring for and restoring leather items for many years.

By following these step-by-step techniques and best practices for leather care, you can ensure that your leather projects remain in excellent condition, preserve their beauty, and last for years. Proper care and maintenance enhance the longevity of your leather creations and showcase your craftsmanship and dedication as a skilled leatherworker.

Conclusion

In this concluding chapter of Leatherworking 101, we express heartfelt gratitude for the inspiring journey we've shared. From delving into leather types to Leather care and maintenance, you have become a skilled and confident leather artisan. Let's celebrate your achievements and bid farewell with a renewed passion for leatherworking and boundless creativity.

Let's dive into them:

Recap of what we have Covered

As we conclude this comprehensive guide to Leatherworking 101, let's take a moment to reflect on the incredible ground we've covered together. Throughout this journey, you have acquired a wealth of knowledge and skills that have transformed you into a skilled and confident leather artisan.

- We began with a deep dive into the diverse world of leather types. You explored the unique qualities of each type, understanding how they influence the appearance, durability, and texture of your creations. With this knowledge, you can confidently select the perfect leather for each project, ensuring your pieces stand out with style and resilience.

- Next, we armed you with an essential arsenal of leatherworking tools. From cutting implements like knives and shears to precision tools like awls and groovers, you became well-versed in each tool's purpose and proper use. You can now approach your leatherworking projects with precision, efficiency, and the confidence to tackle even the most intricate designs.

- Creating an organized and inspiring workspace was our next focus. By setting up your leather workshop thoughtfully and arranging tools and materials carefully, you cultivated an environment that fosters creativity and productivity. Your workspace is now a sanctuary for your creative pursuits, providing the perfect backdrop for bringing your ideas to life.

- With a solid foundation, we immersed ourselves in the heart of leatherworking techniques. You mastered the art of cutting, stitching, and tooling, skillfully bringing your designs to fruition. The step-by-step guides served as your trusted companions, guiding you through each process with meticulous detail. Your craftsmanship has flourished, and the creations that emerge from your hands now boast a level of artistry that is uniquely yours.

- Beyond the art of creation, we have emphasized caring for your leather goods. You learned how to protect, clean, and maintain your leather pieces, ensuring they age gracefully and retain their beauty for years. Understanding proper care and maintenance is essential in preserving the beauty and longevity of your creations.

Acknowledgment

As you reflect on the knowledge and skills acquired throughout this journey, remember that you are no longer just a beginner. You have become a leather artisan who can transform raw materials into exquisite art pieces. Your passion, dedication, and willingness to learn have led you to this point, and the possibilities for your future leatherworking endeavors are boundless.

Heartfelt Gratitude

I am immensely grateful for your presence and dedication on this leatherworking journey as we come to the final pages. It has been an incredible privilege to be your guide as you explore the fascinating world of leather crafting.

Thank you for choosing this guide as your companion in leatherworking. Your commitment to learning and growing as a leather artisan has been inspiring. Your enthusiasm and

eagerness to embrace each chapter's challenges and opportunities have made this guide successful.

Closing Remarks

As you come to the end of this guide, know that you carry the potential to create extraordinary works of art through leatherworking. Your dedication, perseverance, and love for the craft are the fuel that propels you forward on this artistic path.

May your creative spirit continue to shine brightly in all that you create. As you step into the boundless possibilities that await you, I wish you fulfillment, success, and the joy of crafting beautiful leather pieces that resonate with your artistic soul.

Happy crafting, and may your path be marked with endless inspiration and artistic triumphs. Farewell, and may your creative endeavors be nothing short of extraordinary!

As you venture forth, know you are not alone on this creative path. You are part of a vibrant and supportive community of fellow leatherworkers, all united by the love of craftsmanship. Engage, share, and collaborate with others, for you can elevate the art of leatherworking to new and awe-inspiring heights.

Celebrate every triumph, big or small, as a testament to your dedication and talent. Each project is a stepping stone towards honing your skills and unlocking your vast potential.

I do not doubt that your future as a leather artisan will be filled with fulfillment, success, and boundless inspiration. Your creativity can touch lives, bring beauty to the world, and leave a lasting legacy of your artistry.

So, my fellow leather artisan, I leave you with the warmest wishes for a journey filled with wonder, growth, and unyielding passion for leatherworking. Let the joy of creating with your hands be a guiding light that leads you to new artistic horizons.

May your creativity flow freely, may your passion burn brightly, and may your path be adorned with masterpieces that reflect the brilliance of your artistic soul.

Happy crafting, and may your leatherworking endeavors be nothing short of remarkable. Farewell, and may your artistic spirit soar to greater heights with each creation you bring to life!

www.ingramcontent.com/pod-product-compliance
Lightning Source LLC
La Vergne TN
LVHW091120080826
845145LV00008B/1996

* 9 7 8 1 9 5 1 7 3 7 5 8 0 *